PHOENIX RISING

A MEMOIR

Gloria Fung Chee Chou

Dedication

To my mother for her model of courage, strength,
and the love of freedom, and for her self-sacrificing "Yes!"
that gave me the chance to live in the land of freedom.

To my father for spending his life working to provide
for his family's physical and spiritual needs,
and for saving me from drowning so I could see my amazing life
through to its natural conclusion.

Memories of Home

I WAS BORN on the 30th day of the fourth month in the Chinese lunar calendar, or June 25, 1931, by the Western calendar. The place where I was born was a two-story L-shaped building across from a four-story factory building in the city of Tsingtao, China. (Many years later Chairman Mao renamed Tsingtao; it is now called Qingdao.) My parents, who had already produced three daughters, were disappointed that I was not their long-desired son. My mother was near the end of her child-bearing years, and my parents had desperately wanted a son.

My nickname for the first few years of my life was Ling Dee, which meant "Bring a younger brother." My three sisters, however, called me Do Zeu, which translates as "Little Pea." When I entered kindergarten, I was registered as Chou Fung Chee, which means "Phoenix Rising." That remains my official name.

When I was a toddler two of my sisters, the second and third daughters, contracted meningitis. The second daughter died; the third daughter survived but lost the vision in her left eye.

My earliest vivid memory is of an ocean trip when I was three years old. We sailed north to Dalien, where my paternal grandparents lived on a farm. It was my first time on a farm, and it must have been summer because I remember vines laden with big purple grapes. Farm animals were numerous, and although I could not name them all, I could smell them, and I objected loudly to the odor, pinching my nose and crying, "Cho, cho," which means "stinky."

Before we left the farm, our departure possibly hastened by my loud objections to the animal smells, my grandfather gathered the family around the kitchen table and opened a large book to a page recording the Chou lineage. My grandfather was a first son of his generation and had produced eight sons himself. My father was a first son as well. Under his name in the book, however, were only blank spaces where sons would have been listed.

Despite my being a disappointment to him initially, mine was a loving father. He often took time away from his work to drive us to the beach for family outings. It was on one of these occasions, when I was five years old, that he saved me from drowning.

My mother was a second-generation Christian, and together with her sister she had gone into the countryside to convert the villagers. Eventually, my mother persuaded my father to accept Christianity as his religion. His conversion caused him to understand we are all God's children—boys and girls alike.

My parents attended evening church services three times a week. My third sister and I could choose whether to accompany them or stay at home. (My eldest sister stayed home because she had homework to do for school.) We usually chose to go to church with our parents because we wanted to ride in my father's Model A Ford. We typically brought our doll case and played in the back of the church. The adults sang, and we occasionally joined in, because we often sang the same hymns at home, with my mother at the pump organ.

My father worried that it would not be easy to find a good husband for his third daughter, who was handicapped by her partial blindness. He believed she could find a good life with a Christian community. In accordance with that belief, he had a U-shaped single-story building constructed around the church. This building was designed to house communal apartments and provide a Christian home for my sister. He was a good and thoughtful provider, and when he died of a brain tumor (I was six years old at the time), he left his wife and three daughters comfortably well provided for, spiritually and financially.

Sand Castle

I STILL HAVE in my possession a black and white photograph from 1936, showing me at age five and my sister Bi Yuen, age seven, sitting under a ginkgo tree. We have short-cropped hair with bangs in front. A row of storage buildings marches out of the picture on the right, and behind us loom piles of wooden planks. Looking at this picture still evokes memories of the pungent smell of phosphorus from my father's match factory. Bi Yuen and I are sitting in the stock yard of the factory, facing Baba's office, which is an extension of our living quarters.

It was a midsummer day. We had finished our daily calligraphy lesson with Mama. The clear blue sky and gentle breeze invited us to play outdoors, and the thought of being at the seashore pulled at us. We loved the beach. We convinced ourselves that our father probably had not noticed the fog had lifted and would surely want to leave his stuffy office for the sea air.

Waiting for Baba to take us to the beach.

We lingered in front of my father's office, but neither of us wanted to be the first to go inside. The door was partly open. Finally, Bi Yuen stuck her head in and stammered out our wish. "Baba, it's such a nice day. Will you drive us to the beach?"

He looked up from his desk, scratching his crew-cut head, refocusing his eyes on us, and looked out the window. "Look, those leaves are quivering, just like you shiver when you come out of the sea on a cool day," he said. "As soon as the wind stops and not a single leaf is moving, we will go to the beach."

We went out to the ginkgo tree and held its trunk as firmly as we could, trying to still its movement, until our arms became tired, but the leaves continued to quiver. We plopped ourselves down on the ground and waited. Baba snapped our picture from his office window.

Later that same summer, Baba announced at breakfast one day that he would like to spend the entire day at the beach with the family—Mama, Fung Ying, Bi Yuen, and me. The mere mention of the beach caused me to flap my arms as if I were a seagull ready to take off into the sky or skid over the surface of the sea. I could almost hear the sound of the breakers crashing against the rocks and smell the seaweed. Everyone scurried around to gather beachwear. Since I knew Mama would take care of my needs, I was the first one ready and waiting at the top of the stairs, still pretending to be a seagull.

When we reached the beach, the tide was in. Baba decided that at five I was old enough to have proper swimming lessons. He taught me to dog paddle and to hold my breath while dipping my face into the water. After some time he left me to practice with my sisters, using an inner tube.

In the afternoon the tide receded, exposing sea creatures of all sorts. I saw hermit crabs carrying their homes on their backs as they scurried along and crabs that disappeared into the sand when I tried to catch them. I especially enjoyed searching for sea anemones in the crevices of rocks. I would put a finger in the center, which I learned was their mouth, and the soft membrane would fold around my finger.

Years later, when I taught biology in America's Midwest, I was surprised that most of my students had never touched any of those sea creatures alive. Their experiences were limited to the preserved specimens in the laboratory. For Bi Yuen and me these were our seashore friends.

When she picked up a sea star, almost dried up, Bi Yuen said, "Let's build a sand castle with a pool inside to save the stranded sea stars and other creatures." Soon we became so engrossed in our architectural project that we did not notice the rising tide until it reached our castle walls.

"Hurry, hurry, we need to get dry sand and stones to protect our castle," Bi Yuen shouted at me.

My feet kept sinking into the wet sand. Even when I slipped on the seaweed, I made sure that my fists were holding tightly to the dry sand. I did not want to be scolded by my sister. Suddenly, the sand under me gave way and a big wave pulled me into the sea. Water rushed into my nostrils and pressed on my eardrums. I felt as if I were swallowing the whole ocean.

I am not sure how long I was in the water. The next thing I was aware of was that I was in the firm grip of my father's hands. I immediately opened my fists to look for dry sand. My own hands were washed clean and empty, but in my father's loving hands, I was safe. In later years whenever I have come across the words from Isaiah, "I have held you in the palm of my hands," my heart brims with gratitude as I remember my father's saving me from drowning that day and his loving care as he watched over me and the rest of the family.

My father (Baba)

Refugees Out West

WHEN I WAS SIX years old, the safety and security of my childhood began to crumble bit by bit. I became aware of hushed and worried conversations between my parents. I heard the Japanese had kidnapped General Chiang Kai-shek, a Christian like us, and had begun to occupy Tsingtao (Qingdao). (The Japanese occupation of Shandong Province was complete in 1938.) My father was worried about the increased presence of the Japanese in Tsingtao and around his factory. And then Baba began to seem ill. He was thinner, and he started to walk with a limp.

A major blow came when my mother hesitantly told the three of us that our Baba had a brain tumor and we would travel to Jinan to see a specialist there. We would stay with Mama's eldest sister, Big Aunt, but Mama worried about our schooling when we would be far from home.

Fung Ying, the eldest of us three children, spoke up. "I'll bring all my books. I'll help Bi Yuen with her studies and Big Aunt can tutor me. Cousin Jing Ling loves reading stories with Do Zeu." And thus it was decided. We were instructed to bring clothes for every season, an indication that we could not know how long our exile would last. As Mama said, "We need to prepare for whatever God has in store for us."

The train trip to Jinan took less than a day. We girls shared the only spare room in Big Aunt and Big Uncle's small home and slept together in one bed while Mama stayed in the hospital with Baba. All around the bed in which we slept our suitcases stood only partly unpacked. At dinner the night we arrived, Big Uncle said, ominously, "It's good that you are all here. If things get worse, we may have to flee from the Japanese." He was right; less than two days after we arrived, Big Aunt called us together and announced that we must pack quickly to move west, away from the Japanese.

"Is Baba well enough to travel?" Fung Ying asked.

"No, he is too sick to leave. Your Mama will stay with him until he is stronger."

We were allowed to visit our parents in the hospital before we left. We stood at the foot of the bed in which Baba lay propped up by pillows. He motioned for us to come closer, touched each of us on the head, and murmured a blessing.

Very early next morning, in a downpour of rain, Big Aunt, Big Uncle, their son Jing Ling, and we three sisters squeezed into a taxi and were dropped off at the train station where people and luggage jammed the entrance. "Hold on to each other; don't get separated," Big Uncle shouted as he picked me up and held me under one arm.

We boarded the train and found we had only two seats for the six of us. Bi Yuen and I sat on the laps of our aunt and uncle. Fung Ying and Jing Ling took turns sitting on our big suitcase in the aisle. Our parents had come to see us off, Baba leaning on a crutch and Mama helping him stand. The sight of the two of them, leaning together in the drenching rain, waving us out of sight, created an indelible vision in my mind. For the first time I began to realize that my parents could not guarantee my happiness.

I slept through much of that railway journey, waking only to eat or go to the toilet, which was a hole in the floor of a cubicle through which I could see the tracks when I squatted.

We arrived at last in Xian, where we stayed with a business associate of my father before traveling on to Chongqing. Although Big Aunt told us our accommodation was a house for the wealthy, it was a crude dwelling by our standards. Straw mats served as rugs covering the hard-packed mud floor. Running water and electricity had not reached this part of China yet. The toilet was an outhouse.

After about a month, Big Aunt gave her command again, "Pack up your things. Tomorrow we will take a train ride to catch a ship up the Yangtze River to Chongqing."

I was not looking forward to another train ride, but I was excited about sailing on a ship. Two years earlier I had taken an ocean trip with Baba, and I had happy memories of our time together.

Now, however, when I saw the boat that would carry us to Chengdu, my heart sank. It was an old wooden boat. Boards on the gangplank were missing, and the boards on the deck were in even worse condition. "Mama would be shocked by all this dirt," I thought.

Our family of six was assigned to a single bunk. A man in the bunk above ours offered to let me share his space. No sooner had I climbed into the bunk, however, than I was covered with fleas. Big Aunt had to strip me and discard all my clothes.

On the second day, my cousin Jing Ling and Bi Yuen decided to explore the boat. I tagged along. We climbed steep steps with only a rope handrail. The top deck was surround by only a rope railing. Looking down, I got dizzy watching the river pass swiftly beneath the boat. A jolt nearly tossed me off the slippery deck. Either Jing Ling or Bi Yuen pulled me back to safety. (They later disagreed about who the rescuer was.)

Shortly before we reached our destination, the Yangtze River passed through the narrow Sammen Gorge, and we had to transfer to another boat. Above the gorge, small houses and rice fields clung to the steep banks on both sides of the river. (As I write this, many years later, China is building a giant dam to produce hydroelectric power, and the government is forcibly relocating people who had lived along the riverbank for generations.)

Lifeboats were lowered into the water and passengers crowded into them. These lifeboats then struggled through the turbulent water of the gorge, and the passengers, including the six of us, boarded another boat for the conclusion of our journey.

At last we arrived in Chonqing, in Sichuan Province. It was another ancient storybook city. The house we occupied there was constructed of bamboo; even the furniture was bamboo. The city was located in such steep terrain that many of the streets were not streets at all but consisted of broad steps. Buses, cars, and rickshaws were useless in these streets. The most common vehicles were bicycles and sedan chairs carried by two men.

Our school was a short distance down the hill from home. Although we sometimes rode to school in a sedan chair, my sister and I often made a game of the walk to school by jumping over alternate steps and skipping down the slope.

The dialect of the Province of Sichuan sounded like a foreign language to us. We kept our mouths shut and our ears open until we had learned the basics. I made friends with a local girl and began going to and from school with her, learning her dialect.

The Japanese had taken possession of most of central and eastern China. Chiang Kai-shek had escaped from his kidnappers, and he and his government were pushed to their last retreat in Chongqing. Day and night warplanes roared overhead, and occasionally we heard bombs exploding. We thought we had fled to safety; instead we found ourselves at the center of the most strategic target zone of the enemy, while Eastern China, where our journey had begun, was relatively peaceful.

War did not stop Big Aunt from sending us to school. For her and Mama, education was second only to God. During this turbulent period we spent part of nearly every day having lessons in what we called "the cave," which was an air-raid shelter. My teacher accustomed herself to speaking in the pauses between planes and sirens. Between her interrupted speech and my difficulty with the Sichuan dialect, I remember little of my schooling in Chongqing.

Even more important than our schooling in Big Aunt's hierarchy was our commitment to God. We prayed harder than ever during our time in Chongqing, especially during anxious situations. Big Aunt, like her younger sister my mother, took the lead in prayer. Their father had become a Christian when he attended medical school run by American missionaries, and the sisters had grown up as Christians. Baba and Big Uncle were converts through the influence of their wives.

Big Aunt's mantra was, "God is always with us." Prayer was a source of comfort even though some of the words troubled me. For example, when we recited Psalm 23, "The Lord is my Shepherd, I shall not want," I wanted to shout, "I DO want! I want Baba and Mama!" Of course I shouted silently, inside myself. As the youngest daughter in a traditional Chinese family, I learned early that some truths were to be kept in the silence of my heart.

My Father's Death

MY SILENT SHOUT became a wail during the Lunar New Year, 1937. This time, typically a 15-day period of festivities, was cut short by the news of Baba's death. Big Aunt called us to her room. On her bed were three long white robes, each with a black armband. Between sobs she said, "God has taken your Baba home to heaven. Take off your New Year dresses and put on these."

"Will we go back for the funeral?" Fung Ying asked.

"No, it took a month for the letter to reach us. He is already buried, and your mama is on her way here."

White is the color of mourning in China. We wore our white mourning robes with the black armbands until school resumed and then continued to wear the black bands for one year, as was the custom for the mourning of a parent. Only the prospect of being reunited with Mama helped ease the pain of losing Baba to God.

It took Mama nearly two months to reach us in Chonqing after my father's death. Although Mama was in her early forties, she had aged in the few months we had been parted, and there were streaks of gray in her blue-black hair.

Shortly after she arrived, Mama told us about the day our Baba died. She had been sitting near his bed as he hovered between sleep and wakefulness. Suddenly, he sat up and got out of bed. After steadying himself, Baba began to sing psalms from the *Bible*. His face was radiant as he sang and danced around the room. Mama thought she was dreaming. After a time, Baba went back to bed, lay down, stopped breathing, and died, with a slight smile on his face.

Mama (Lin Tsing Mae, Clear Plum)

MY MOTHER was the strongest influence in my life. After the death of my father, she continued heroically to take care of her family, her home, and her husband's business. She has continued to influence me and to give me strength throughout my life. She herself came from a strong family.

Mama was born at the turn of the 20th century in a village outside of Tsinan (now Jinan) in the province of Shantung (now Shandong), the province where Confucius was born. She had one sister, two years her senior. Their father (my maternal grandfather) was a doctor of medicine in both Eastern and Western tradition, which was unusual in China at that time. Because of his education and his wisdom, he was both feared and respected by the people of the village. My grandfather had been educated by missionaries who operated the medical school he attended, and he became a Christian, another rarity among the villagers. As a Christian, he had only one wife. Unfortunately, that one wife committed suicide, and it was Mama who found her mother hanging by a rope in the basement of the family home. (Family members later speculated that the extreme oppression of women by the imperial family led to my grandmother's suicide.)

Grandfather remarried, and his new wife was only four years older than Mama's older sister. The only words Mama could remember this new wife's saying were, "Don't bother me," and "Go away."

Mama and her sister did go away. Grandfather decided they would go to school. The schoolmaster was shocked, as it was unheard of at that time for girls to go to school. Since there were no laws against it, however, my grandfather got his way.

After the boys got over their shock at having two girls in their classes, they began to taunt Mama and her sister, shouting, "What ugly feet!" The standard of beauty in those days was three-inch "golden lilies," or bound feet. This was one more way in which Grandfather was a nonconformist. "No daughter of mine is going to hop around like a chicken," he said.

During the girls' last four years of school, the family moved to Beijing, where both daughters completed teacher training. By that time the revolution led by Sun-Yat-Sen was raging against Empress Qing, and the family found itself in a hotbed of unrest. Mama saw the suffering of the common people in direct contrast to the extravagances of the imperial family and their entourage. Mama and her sister secretly joined the Revolutionary Daughters of the Republic.

One day the revolutionaries planned to stage a protest march, and the two sisters were about to leave the house to join the march when their father came home. Seeing their unbraided hair, which he knew was a symbol of rebellion, Grandfather forbade them to leave the house, even though he too supported the Revolution. Since many of the protest marchers were summarily executed that day, Grandfather probably saved the lives of his daughters.

In the early 1920s Mama was offered a teaching job in Qingdao, where she met and married Baba. Although Baba was uneducated and was not a Christian, Mama used money from her teaching salary to pay his passage to Japan where he attended a technical school. On his return she introduced him to Christianity, and the church he had built near the family home was a sign of his devoutness. Mama's dream had been fulfilled. She had a husband with job skills, who shared her faith.

By 1949 the Communists had "liberated" all of China, and step by step everything the family owned was confiscated. Despite the difficult circumstances, Mama was satisfied that her three daughters were blessed with the three wishes she had for them. Those wishes were 1. That they have all the education their minds could hold; 2. That they would always have God in their hearts; and 3. That they would enjoy health as long as God permits. She knew no one could take those things away from them.

Clear Plum died in 1967, the first year of the Cultural Revolution.

Return to Qingdao

MAMA STAYED in Chongqing just long enough to recuperate from her long trip. One evening I overheard an argument between her and her elder sister. The source of the argument became clear when Mama opened the door and said, "Go get your sisters. We need to get ready to go home."

"Go home! Go home to Qingdao?" I cheered.

Our return trip was considerably more comfortable and less stressful than our exodus, except at the border of Annam, which is now known as Vietnam, where there was a problem about the amount and type of currency Mama carried. As we huddled around her in the customs office at the train station, I remember Mama's firm hand holding mine, her lips moving in prayer. The

Mama and three girls return to Qingdao after Baba's death.
(L to R: Do Zeu, Mama, Fung Ying, Bi Yuen)

authorities threatened to confiscate all her money. Finally, after she paid a large fine, we were allowed to catch the next train across the Yunnan province to the coast. I don't know how long it took the ship to cross to Hong Kong, but it seemed much faster, because the atmosphere was calm, and the ship was spacious.

The lines on Mama's brow loosened up. After prayer one evening she wanted to have a family talk. She said, "Your Baba thought of you girls up to the last days of his life. He ordered a house to be built for us next to the home of the Tsous. Your Baba worked hard for you."

Mama also said, "We won't travel to Qingdao right away. I need time to think about whom I could ask to manage your Baba's financial affairs." It was unthinkable at the time for a woman in China to take over her deceased husband's business.

She rented an apartment in Kowloon and set up temporary residence. Fung Ying was sent to a boarding school in Hong Kong. Bi Yuen and I had home schooling with Mama.

Mama had taught me at an early age, as soon as I was able to manipulate a pair of chopsticks, how to hold a brush dipped in black ink, and how to trace over red Chinese characters in a workbook. Having a parent who had been a teacher could transform our home instantly into a school.

We stayed in Kowloon for almost a year. After Lunar New Year, Mama received word that our house was nearly ready for occupancy. She waited another two months to book passage to Qingdao. Fung Ying remained in Hong Kong until school closed in June.

"A real ship!" Bi Yuen and I jumped for joy, as we stood on the dock. The ship was a British ocean liner, and we had our very own cabin! We could watch the waves, the seagulls, and the floating clouds through a porthole in our cabin. The dining room tables were set with white cloths and napkins under the silverware and chopsticks.

Mr. and Mrs. Tsou met us when we arrived, with the news that there had been some unexpected delay in the completion of our house. "In the meantime, please accept our humble home as yours," Mr. Tsou said.

The next day, Mama opened several suitcases without really unpacking. As soon as she found the dresses she needed for herself, my sister Bi Yuen, and me, she said, "I want you to look your very best. We are going to visit schools." After we finished dressing, she scrutinized us from head to foot, then combed and re-braided our hair. By the end of the day we were registered in St. Joseph Elementary School, Bi Yuen in grade 4 and I in grade 2. "Too bad it's a Catholic school, not a Jesu Jiao (Protestant)," Mama sighed, but I also heard a note of pride in her voice for her successful school hunt.

We were now looking forward to resuming a normal life. Fung Ying would soon come back from Hong Kong. In the fall, she would enter ninth grade at St. Joseph Middle School, and we would live in our new home, perhaps forever.

The Tsous had three sons and two daughters. Mrs. Tsou was head wife, but Mr. Tsou also had a second wife, who with her two daughters lived in the same house. Fortunately, the three-story house had sufficient space to accommodate this large family.

Above the third floor was a space filled entirely by a shrine. There were statues of Lao-tze, Kungfuzu (Confucius), Guan-yin, Buddha, Mohammed, and Jesus. (The seven girls then living together at the Tsous were all considered "daughters," albeit from different women.) The youngest, number seven daughter, and I used to sneak up to the shrine and play imaginary games with the gods. We coveted the offerings of fresh food provided for them, but we knew enough to resist the temptation; the punishment for sampling those offerings would be much more serious than just reaching into a cookie jar.

An Arranged Marriage

IN THE TENTH MONTH of lunar year 1924, Fung Ying was born, and a month later the Tsous sent red-colored hard boiled eggs to our family to announce the birth of their second son, Lai Yu. The two families had decided before the birth of the babies that, if one was a girl and the other a boy, they would be betrothed. I remember seeing a photo in our family album showing two chubby babies propped up by pillows in an upholstered chair. Each wore a jade medallion. That was their engagement photo.

During their growing up years, Fung Ying and Lai Yu saw each other whenever the two families visited each other, maybe once a year. Fung Ying did not look forward to those visits. She became unusually quiet a few days before the visit and was very animated after the visit ended. The children from both families learned never to tease either of them by saying, "There's your fiancé."

When Fung Ying came back from Hong Kong after the end of the school year in June of 1938, Mama, Bi Yuen, and I were still guests at the Tsous, waiting for the completion of our own house. Bi Yuen and Lai Yu were young teenagers now, and they were going to be neighbors, not just friends across town. The realization dawned that if they were going to share lives together in the future, they had better begin to find common threads to weave a life harmoniously. Mama already had this in mind when she found a good boys' school for Lai Yu and his brothers.

Lai Yu himself, looking for a common interest in music, began taking violin lessons after he learned that Fung Ying had been playing the piano at the academy in Hong Kong. After we moved into our own house, I remember seeing Lai Yu, through the window of his house, practicing on his violin. After high school, they both attended the Catholic University in Beijing, where he played in the university orchestra as first violinist. Fung Ying chose home economics as her major, and Lai Yu chose economics.

With all the efforts their parents made to ensure they were a perfect match, there must have been moments of doubt. Arranged marriages were no longer as common in my generation as they had been in my parents' time. Certainly the fact of their engagement was not something that won the two students any popularity points at the university.

I remember one day in summer, after Fung Ying's first year in Beijing, when she and Mama were arguing in Mama's bedroom. Their voices became louder and louder. Soon they opened the door, and Mama told Bi Yuen and me that they were going to take a walk on the beach. After they left the house Bi Yuen said, "I bet Zia-Zia (elder sister) met a boy at university and wants to break the engagement."

Without actually hearing their conversation, we could imagine Mama pointing to the stack of carved camphor chests in the corner of her room, filled with yards and yards of silk and other precious objects. "I've been preparing for your wedding ever since you were born. Besides how can we break the news to the Tsous? What would others say? Your Baba would turn over in his grave!"

When Mama and Fung Ying came home, we knew who had won. "Poor Zia Zia," Bi Yuen whispered to me, "I hope Mama never gets the crazy idea to engage either one of us."

"Me too," I echoed.

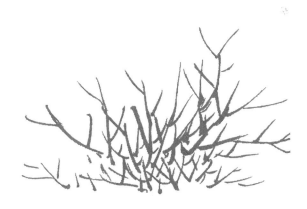

St. Joseph School

I WAS EIGHT YEARS old when I entered second grade at St. Joseph School. The language of instruction in good Chinese schools was Mandarin. People in Qingdao spoke the Shandong dialect, which was very similar to Mandarin since Beijing (where Mandarin originated) is located in the neighboring province of Hebei. Bi Yuen and I spoke the Shandong dialect, with a touch of Sichuan dialect, and Cantonese, which was spoken in Hong Hong and Kowloon. Visitors passing open windows of the classrooms of the primary grades at St. Joseph School would hear the children's singsong four-tone recitation. Using an incorrect tone could cause misunderstanding, or laughter, as frequently occurred with foreigners. Many of the missionaries I knew were proficient in the language, but only two had mastered the proper tones.

I was quick to master the Mandarin and I was able to do so for two reasons. First, I had a good and caring teacher, and second, I wanted to avoid peer disapproval. I had a much more difficult time, however, learning Japanese, mastery of which was mandated by the ruling government. All official Japanese documents used Chinese characters; even elementary levels of the language included some Chinese characters. This fact did not enhance my interest in learning the enemy's language. Years later, when I needed to learn English and French, as well as Japanese again, I realized that emotions play a strong role in learning a new language.

I also had private piano lessons at this time, during which I enjoyed the full attention of my teacher, Sister Fides. She used to come for me during the school day for my piano lessons. I dropped hints hoping she might schedule my lessons during Japanese language classes, but to no avail. Bi Yuen had the same hope for timing her violin lessons. A few times a week we stayed after school to practice our music.

One day when we came back from school, all the suitcases were packed.

"Are we going to flee again as refugees?" I asked.

"No," Mama assured me. "But we're going to live in a hotel until our house is ready. I refuse to be dictated to by the in-laws." That was the end of our life with the Tsous.

After we got settled in our latest temporary home, Mama told us that for Mr. Tsou, who had two wives, she was just another lowly woman. Little did he know that this woman almost lost her head during the last days of Empress Qing, because of her independent spirit. Fung Ying told me this story many years later.

We managed to live fairly normal lives in spite of the Japanese Occupation.

Before the end of the school term, Bi Yuen and I begged Mama for a bicycle each. "Whoever ends up the year in the top three of her class will get a bicycle," she replied. We swallowed hard. There were about 50 students in each class. That would be a nearly impossible goal for two girls who had been schooled at home and for a brief period under very stressful conditions in Chongqing.

The day the school reports arrive in the mail, Mama was not home. We carefully unsealed the envelope so we could re-seal it undetected. I was in the upper third of my grade, but not in the top three; Bi Yuen had managed to achieve sixth place in her grade. We knew Mama would not lower her standards when it came to eduation. Bi Yuen came up with a plan to change her report card. I was old enough to know we would both be in deep trouble if Mama found out. "Let's just try harder next school year," I urged.

"No. I've worked really hard and I deserve to have the bicycle now. When I get it, I'll teach you how to ride." Bi Yuen then painstakingly erased the "6" and replaced it with a "3," sealed the envelope, and returned it to the pile of the day's mail.

After an agonizing wait, we heard Mama's footsteps on the stairs. We pretended to be totally engrossed in a game. After another seemingly long delay, Mama called us and showed us our report cards. My heart was pounding so hard I could hardly hear my sister remind Mama of her promise. The next week, Mama called Fifth Uncle (Baba had been the eldest of eight sons and one daughter) and asked him to select the best bicycle for a 10-year-old girl When he delivered the promised bike, I was disappointed to discover my legs were too short to reach the pedals, but Bi Yuen asked Fifth Uncle to attach two bars, one on either side of the central screw of the back wheel so she could let me stand on the bars and hold onto her shoulders as she cycled.

The bicycle came in handy during summer vacation. We could reach the beach in 10 minutes, half the time it took us to walk. When the weather was warm enough to swim, we planned to spend most of our days on the beach.

How wrong we were! Mama made sure our brains were not on vacation. There were calligraphy lessons, music lessons, and practice times. As I got older, she added simplified martial arts, typing, and studying the Chinese classics. Nevertheless, I remember my summers as carefree days in the company of my siblings, neighbors, and friends.

Sister George

THE TEACHING STAFF of St. Joseph School consisted of Chinese teachers, American Sisters, and two Chinese Sisters, one of whom was Sister George, who taught grade three. Sister Blanda, an American, was the principal of the elementary school. Maybe she did make some efforts in learning to speak Chinese, but as I recall, she primarily spoke English. One time the entire student body of Siao Shwugh (small school, grades one to six) was summoned to the courtyard. Sister Blanda stood on the stone steps that led to the Jone Shwugh (middle school). She had a ruler in one hand, and as she proceded to speak, she slapped her other hand with the ruler for emphasis. Her face was red, and she shouted. I did not know if she was speaking English or Chinese, since I knew no English, but she was clearly very angry.

When we returned to our own classrooms, Sister George told us a student had been caught stealing. I understood then the reason for the ruler. It was to be used on the culprit's hands. "Of course I know none of you would even think of taking someone else's things," Sister George said, as she looked at us like a trusting mother who loved her children.

Grade three was the most memorable of my small school years. I woke every morning eager to get to school. When the school bell rang, all the students lined up according to grade, and their teachers stood facing them. The physical education teacher then led us in 15 minutes of calisthenics. We did these exercises in all seasons and all kinds of weather before silently following our teachers to our respective classrooms. Later, when I became a teacher in America and looked into the sleepy faces of my students each morning, I recalled the benefits of the Chinese morning exercise.

In retrospect I admire Sister Blanda for her willingness to work with the younger students, which forced her to use the Chinese language, even though she clearly struggled. All the other American Sisters taught in the high middle school, in which the language of instruction was English.

Even though the older students were being instructed in English, the names of the Sisters still seemed strange, so they made up a nickname for each Sister. There was Sister Crooked Neck, Sister Beer Barrel, Sister Pretty, and so on. My teacher's nickname, to my shock, was Sister Ugly. I protested to Fung Ying when she told me. "If you really knew her you'd see she is the most beautiful person of all," I said. If she were judged only by outward appearance, the name Sister Ugly might have had some merit. No one, though, was more respected and loved than Sister George, most of all by her third grade students. Three of the most important decisions of my life were influenced by her charisma.

Sister George invited her students to listen to *Bible* stories on Fridays after school. (No religion was taught during regular school hours.) I always dashed out as soon as we were dismissed so I could find a place close to her chair in the small wooden annex next to the church across the street. I had heard the same *Bible* stories at home since my earliest days. When Mama wondered why I wanted to prolong the school day, I said, "No one tells *Bible* stories like Sister George."

Corpus Christi

TOWARD THE END of the school year, Sister George told us about a big Catholic feast called Corpus Christi, the Body of Christ. On that day, there would be a procession around the Catholic Square. Anyone who wished to participate had to get their parents' permission and attend several classes for explanations and rehearsals.

Mama considered my listening to *Bible* stories harmless, maybe even commendable, but I encountered some resistance when I tried to convince her how important my participation in the Corpus Christi celebration would be. A teacher's words carried a lot of weight with my mother, however, so now she faced a dilemma. Those who wished to be flower girls in the procession had to go through a rehearsal after school and arrive an hour early on the day itself. Although the Corpus Christi celebration went against her Protestant beliefs, Mama's respect for teachers was to be honored, and she gave her consent.

When the big day arrived, I woke up before dawn, waking up the entire household. Mama had had to buy a white fluffy dress for me for the occasion. Sister George waited for us in the annex near the church. She put a white chiffon veil and a crown of flowers on each girl, and gave each of us a basket filled with fragrant petals.

When all the bells in the church steeple rang, we lined up to join the procession. The leader was an altar boy in a red robe covered with a hip-length white top, with lace at the edges of the sleeves and lower hem. He held a stick with a cross on top. About a dozen other altar boys in the same attire followed him two by two. Some held tall candles; others rang bells. Some priests were in black robes and white tops, others wore different colored vestments and walked behind the boys. We entered behind the priests. Two altar boys came in after us, walking backward and swinging their incensors. The procession took place under a large ornate canopy. A priest at each corner held the pole that supported the canopy. The bishop, dressed in an elaborate ceremonial cloak, raised a monstrance, a golden vessel from the center of which radiated golden rays. A white host was visible through the glass in the center. That was the Body of Christ, or Corpus Christi, Sister George had explained during our practice period.

Our job was to sprinkle flower petals in the path of the holder of Corpus Christi. I reached for the soft petals, and threw them into the air and took a deep breath to enjoy the sweet fragrance. Five outdoor altars were set up. The procession stopped at each one, where a ritual was performed, at the end of which the bishop turned toward the people and blessed them with the monstrance. I did not understand any of his prayers, which were in Latin, but I loved the strange-sounding music.

Our last stop was at the main altar in the Cathedral. As we entered, music from the pipe organ in the loft filled that immense space, and the smell of beewax from huge candles permeated the air. The altar boys, the priests, and the bishop in their colorful clothing surrounded the altar. When we reached our pew, each of us genuflected on one knee before taking our places. Sister George had practiced with us, and I had practiced at home so as not to stumble on the great day itself.

Mama got quite an earful about Corpus Christi as I described the colorful ceremonial garb, the smells, the organ music, the pageantry. At the next *Bible* class, Sister George told us we were welcome to attend Mass every Sunday, not just on special feast days.

Mama's response to my request to go to more Sunday Masses did not match my eagerness to do so. She said, "You know we always go to our church on Sundays as a family." When I begged her to make an exception for one more time, she gave her consent. As it turned out, I went more than once. Ordinary Sundays were not like Corpus Christi, but within that space I often felt as if I were transported to another place and time. Sometimes during High Mass I had a sense of my own boundaries fading, that I was expanding with the choir and organ music. Maybe it was a child's sense of the holy. Sermons, though, created tense moments for me. I rarely understood the message.

Once in a while a foreign priest used the incorrect tone for a word, creating a different meaning. This mistake would start a ripple of giggles among us students, and Sister George would look down the pew with a disapproving frown. To avoid future fits of giggles, I tried to keep my mind elsewhere during sermons.

Close to the end of the school year, I found my mother sitting on the couch reading. I sat down next to her and stammered, "Mama, I have a big favor to ask you." She must have thought that I wanted to attend another Mass and I had just gone last Sunday. I suddenly blurted out, "I want to be a Catholic, like Sister George." Her patience had reached its limit. I could almost read her thoughts, which would be something like this: "I have been Protestant for two generations, and your father became a convert because of me. I want you children to carry my faith to the fourth generation and beyond. Even if I value independence and have encouraged it in my children, this is not what I had in mind."

After composing herself she took off her reading glasses and looked intently at me, "You are only nine years old. You are too young to think about such an important decision. When you are older and can answer all my questions to my complete satisfaction about the Catholic religion, we'll talk about it."

From that moment I dedicated all my free time to learning everything I could about Catholicism. Sister George found me at her desk constantly. Even after I had moved beyond grade three, she always greeted me with a warm smile whenever I popped into her classroom after school. She lent me books to read. Even though most were beyond my reading level, I devoured them zealously. I decided not to bring up the subject with Mama again, but I believe that ever since the day I first raised the question of becoming a Catholic, Mama did not drop the subject from her mind. She had been thinking and perhaps reading about the Catholic church. She thought Catholics worshipped idols and statues of Mary, and that they took orders from a foreign leader in Rome. She resented the fact that Protestants were considered heretics by the Catholics.

I was not able to counter Mama's objections, and we had reached a silent stalemate when an earth-changing event occurred in the world. On December 7, 1941, Japan bombed Pearl Harbor. America immediately became the enemy of the Occupation Troop of the Japanese in Qingdao.

A few days after the news of the bombing, when I stopped to see Sister George, she said, "Oh, I'm glad you're here. You must ask your mother about being baptized next Sunday." She explained that the citizens of Japan's enemy countries were given two choices. They must either leave China or go into concentration camps, and the American Sisters had chosen the latter.

Most of the priests would have the same choices. Thus the church would not be able to function as usual.

I decided to risk asking Mama. To my surprise, she did not answer yes or no. She still insisted on an "oral exam," although in a shortened version. I remember observing myself, wondering if that was really me, answering clearly and forcefully some questions that were very complex for a person my age. When Mama paused, my heart was pounding. Years later when I sat for my oral exam in a graduate theology course, Ecclesiology, I remembered this former time. How much it must have cost Mama for her consent I would know only in the years to come.

On December 13, 1941, my baptism took place in St. Michael's Cathedral. All the girls were baptized as Mary—our patron saint—and all the boys were Michael. There were no Chinese saints whose names would be used for us. After the church ceremony, a few of us were called into the sacristy. We had to read and sign a formal statement "renouncing" our Protestant heresy. I remember feeling a twinge of betrayal to my parents' religion.

Just a week after my hurried baptism, I was in the school playground when the school loudspeaker blared an announcement. "Attention, attention everyone! "This is a very, very important announcement from your principal. Everyone report to your homeroom immediately." Thus our noon recess came to an abrupt end. We brushed the snow from our uniforms and hurried inside. Teacher Han stood at the door of the fourth grade classroom. We moved quickly and quietly to our seats, and she called roll. When she began to speak, her voice had a slight tremor. "As you know, since last week's bombing of Pearl Harbor, we're faced with many changes. Winter holidays will begin a week early. When the bell rings in a few minutes you are dismissed. Do not return until further notice. Make sure that you take all your belongings home. Here's a note for the oldest child of each family." My eldest sister was in senior high school. We students were shocked into silence. My heart was pounding against my ribcage, and a thousand questions jammed and numbed my brain.

For the first time the bell had a hollow ring to it, and no one rushed out. As I stepped ouside my classroom I heard, "Mei-Mei (Little Sister), let's go home." My sister Bi Yuen's sixth-grade room was just two doors down the hall from mine. We were walking from the elementary gate along the high wall toward the high school gate when a large gray military truck screeched to a halt in the street beside us. We covered our mouths and noses to keep out the dust and the suffocating smell of gasoline. Four Japanese soldiers, in uniforms the same color as the truck, emerged. Two of them stomped up the stone steps into the school while two others stayed outside, using bayonets to keep the crowd away from the school entrance and the truck.

Time passed like the beat of a military march. When the front door of the school opened, our twelve American sisters emerged, clad in their floor-length black mantles, each one carrying a bag. Their faces were almost as white as the head dress under their black veils. The last in line, Sister Eustella, the principal, had lost her usual ruddy complexion and warm smile. She raised a hand to wave, but a soldier roughly pushed her into the truck. My sister's mittened hand tightened around mine. The soldiers got into the truck, and the door closed loudly. As the truck drove away, we onlookers broke into open sobs.

Holy Ghost International School

IN JANUARY, 1942, after the Japanese soldiers had taken away many members of the faculty of St. Joseph's School, Mama transferred Bi Yuen and me to Holy Ghost International School, across the street from St. Joseph's. I was 10 years old.

In registering me for school, Mama was asked for my English name. She was stumped. She could only remember that our Fourth Uncle had chosen our Western names—Grace, Gloria, and Mary. "Which one is this?" asked the sister. "All I know is it is one of the ones that begins with G," Mama answered, looking to me for help. I did not know which name was mine, either, so the nun chose the first one on the list and I became Grace. But I was not to keep that name for long.

We also learned that day the language of instruction at Holy Ghost International School was English. Surely Mama must have realized I had barely shaken off the several dialects to which I had been exposed in order to learn Mandarin, not to mention now having to learn Japanese during the Occupation. My English was just about nonexistent.

On the first day of school, I took my place with the youngest students, Form I, which was the Chinese equivalent of grades 1 and 2. (If I had been proficient in English, I should have been in Form II.) My teacher led us into the classroom, where she wrote her name and said, "I am Sister Mary." Sister Mary looked Chinese, and I fleetingly hoped I could converse with her in our language until I learned some English. I was disappointed to learn she was from the Philippines. The only two spoken languages permitted at school were English and French. The nuns and some of the boarding students conversed in French.

I struggled to learn English as quickly as I could, but Sister Mary was more hindrance than help. Every time I mispronounced a word, she banged on her desk or the chalkboard and made me repeat the word over and over until she was satisfied. (Later, when I was a teacher myself, I remembered that fear is the greatest obstacle to learning anything, especially a foreign language.)

My rapid acquisition of English was due to another source. When I was still in Form I, not long after school started, I was standing all alone on the playground when a tall girl approached and introduced herself. In English she said, "My name is Micky. I'm in Form IV." Then she leaned in and whispered to me in Chinese. "I saw you coming out of a house on Roen Chung Road. I live at the other end of the same road. Maybe we could get together some weekend."

Soon after that, Micky and I began to spend every weekend together. She was a Russian Jew. Her grandparents had left Russia during the Bolshevik Revolution. At home she spoke Russian with her family and Chinese with their servants. When we talked, Micky pretended she knew no Chinese, which forced me to speak English and use body language. Micky was kind and gentle in correcting my mistakes, unlike Sister Mary. Sometimes the mistakes I made reduced us both to tears of helpless laughter. With Micky, learning was such fun that I mastered English within five months. Soon I was even able to think in English.

One day when Micky came over to our house, Fung Ying heard her call me Grace. "That's my name!" she announced. "Yours is Gloria!" It was no use trying to make Fung Ying change her English name, because all her American teachers called her by that name. I suffered some embarrassment when I had to stand up after a school assembly and announce that I was now to be called Gloria, not Grace. It took a few days before Micky and I could laugh about the mistake.

After one semester, when my report card indicated I had been promoted to Form II (grades 3 and 4), my first thought was, "Thank you, Micky!" My teacher was short and, in my mind, elderly (although she may not have been much older than Mama), with a narrow face. Western people seem to age differently, I thought, and they even count their age in a different way. (Chinese people are one year old at birth and then advance one year with each lunar year.) I was in her class one year and then moved on to Form III (grades 5 and 6.)

In Form III at last I was in a class with children closer to my age. It was difficult to tell how old my new teacher was, since her habit covered everything but her face and hands. I liked the head dress around her rosy cheeks. It was much looser than the ones worn by the Black Sisters of St. Joseph's School. She wrote her name, "Mother Theonesta," on the chalkboard and told us how to pronounce it.

"Welcome to the nine students from Form II and welcome back to the second-year students," she said. "As your name is called please tell us something about yourself." I was not the only Chinese student, among the seven countries represented in the class. Even if my English was far from fluent, I could detect an accent when Mother Theonesta spoke. She told us she was from a small village in Austria near the Black Forest.

"This summer I spent two lovely weeks in our retreat house in Lao Shan," she said, closing her eyes as if she were remembering the sound of the waterfall, the swaying bamboo groves in the temple gardens, and the curious rock formations. Lao Shan was a few hours from Qingdao by bus, and I had been there with my family. It has been the source of inspiration for some great Chinese poetry and paintings. For the first time, at this school, I did not feel like an odd piece in a puzzle, and I looked forward to a less stressful year. After recess we each received our program of studies. I glanced over mine, pointing to a subject that I thought was an error in scheduling, Mother Theonesta caught my quizzical look. "Now that your English is almost in place, you have to catch up with our foreign language requirement, which is French." I wanted to protest that English was my foreign language, but I knew protest would be useless.

I saved my complaint until I got home. Mama expressed her empathy by arranging private lessons for me to catch up on four years of French, which I had never studied. I studied French as an academic exercise. Even after I had taken this foreign language for many years, all the way through college, only rarely did I ever find myself thinking and speaking in French simultaneously.

Many times my Form III compositions were returned to me with more red ink than blue. I often had to rewrite my assignments several times. Sometimes after the third or fourth time, Mother Theonesta would sit with me after school and go over my lesson word by word, until she was satisfied. Before beginning my remedial work, she would leave and come back with a taffy on a stick for me.

One evening when I was doing my homework at the family table, I turned to asked Mama a question. She usually sat on the couch reading, and I noticed the cover of her current book had both English and Chinese words. Seeing the look on my face, she said, "I've decided to take up English. So far it seems to be easier than German."

"Mama, you're going to start learning a foreign language at your age?" I inquired. (She was not yet 50 years old.) My insensitive question drew a sharp retort. "As long as I have breath, I can learn. Besides, I want to be able to read letters from school and not depend on you to translate." (Secretly, I suspected she also wanted to understand my conversations with my friends.) On another occasion, Mama told me she would stop learning only when she was six feet underground.

Mama's passion for learning found a match in Mother Theonesta. After school, Mama usually prepared a hot snack for me. Once my stomach was happy, we would discuss the day's events. In the past, we enjoyed this activity at a leisurely pace. Something, or someone, this year had added urgency to my life. I gulped down my snack, changed my clothes, and headed for the piano. At first Mama seemed surprised to see me so fired up. Whatever it was, though, she was glad she didn't have to remind me to practice or sit next to me to make sure I did.

There was a logical explanation for my fervor at the piano. One day after our singing class, Mother Theonesta asked me to stay back from recess. She handed me two music books and said, "The school is going to have a musical. You will play the accompaniment. I know that you have had four years of piano lessons. Be prepared to play the opening piece for me next week." Her look of confidence swept aside all of my self-doubts.

When I recall my two years with Mother Theonesta, it seems I grew the way a beanstalk does. Her vocabulary lacked the words "I can't," and she would not accept those words from her students. One time when I forgot and said, "I can't," she covered her ears, but I was sure this time she was being over-confident regarding my abilities.

"In May Reverend Mother is coming from Rome to visit us," she said. "You will give the welcome speech in English and an older student will do it in French." She was not asking me; she was telling me.

When Bi Yuen reached her teens she was a grown woman. My physical changes at 12 and 13 were much slower. In fact Mama worried that I was shorter than both my sisters when they were at that age. She and Fung Ying used to hold opposite ends of my body -- feet and head -- and try to stretch me. I believe my mental growth at this time more than made up for my lack of physical development.

My best friend in Form III was Diana Dormis. She lived with a Japanese mother and was told that her father was an American naval officer, although she had no memories of him. Many children in our school were multiracial. I liked Diana not only because she was shorter than I but because she was a whiz at spelling. When she came over to my house, I made sure Mama noted her diminutive height. We used to play spell-down, using our big dictionary to test each other. Very rarely did Diana make a mistake. No matter how smart a student was, though, Mother Theonesta had a gift for stretching each student to her or his highest potential.

I only appreciated Mother Theonesta fully on the last day of Form III. Convocation it was called. All the teachers came in their formal attire, white woolen garb and veils, no pinafores. They sat on the stage facing the parents, who sat in the main body of the auditorium/gym. Students sat on bleachers on either side. When his or her name was called, a student rose, went to the center front, curtsied or bowed, and remained standing until all the grades on the report card were read out loud by the homeroom teacher, including the student's rank in class. At the end of this procedure, the student would ascend the steps and receive a report card from the headmistress. During the last part of the Convocation, the when awards were given, my name was called so many times that the smile on Mama's face became a fixture. At the conclusion of the formalities, Mama sought out the person she knew was responsible for my success. Mother Theonesta simply pointed to me and said, "Your daughter did it."

Years later when I myself went into the teaching profession, Mother Theonesta and Sister George were my sources of inspiration.

The Pink Sisters

RELIGION WAS ONE area of our lives in which the Occupying Force did not interfere. Father Dahlencum told me about a group of German Sisters, called the Pink Sisters, who had their monastery on a hill not far from my home. They were contemplatives; prayer and manual labor were their way of serving God and the world. The bishop referred to them as the powerhouse of active missionaries. One Sunday, instead of going to the cathedral for mass, I decided to take my bicycle and search out the Pink Sisters. After only about 15 minutes, I had to walk my bicycle the rest of the way up a little path along the side of the hill. Birds chirped in the bushes, and I breathed in fresh air scented with the fragrance of pine trees.

The monastery was a small earth-tone building. The wooden doors were open. I knelt in one of the pews at the rear. An iron railing served as a divider between the visitors' section and that of the Sisters. Compared to St. Michael's Cathedral, this was a simple chapel with only a few stained-glassed windows and statues. A little bell rang as a side door opened to the left. Sisters came through in a silent procession in their pink habits and white veils. Yards and yards of fluffy chiffon covered their faces and trailed behind them. I felt as if I had entered the scene of a fairy tale. "How romantic!" I thought.

Thereafter, I began to attend mass every morning before school, which meant getting up an hour earlier. Mama did not mind the getting up earlier, since she always got up an hour before the family to pray and read the *Bible*. What she did object to was the Eucharistic fast because from mass I went directly to school. She began to include more food than just a snack for my morning recess.

Holy Ghost Convent also had a chapel, which had two separate entrances, one for the nuns and one for outsiders. Often during the noonday recess I would slip into a back pew for a few moments of silence. In the middle of the front, between the first pew of the nuns and the communion railing, was a large, well-padded pew. There was always a nun kneeling there, often gazing fixedly at the monstrance that enclosed the Sacred Host. They practiced perpetual adoration. Every hour around the clock there was the "changing of the guard." Without my realizing it at the time, a deep yearning in my heart was budding and being nurtured.

After Form III I graduated to Form IV, which was taught by Mother Christopher, before moving on the next year to Cambridge Class, which was the equivalent of American high school.

Cambridge Class

THE SOLE PURPOSE of Cambridge Class, which encompassed the entire high school curriculum, was to prepare students to pass their O level and A level exams. These exams were sent to us from Cambridge University in London and proctored by members of the British consulate when we took them. The completed exams were then returned to Cambridge University.

Mother Elfleda was the Cambridge Class tutor. As far as I can remember, she never taught us anything; nor did we have class discussions. Every day we were assigned pages from three of the subjects we needed to master, and the following day we would have to answer a few questions on that material. While the students wrote, Sister Elfleda spent her time knitting baby clothes for the annual bazaar. Next day she would go over the mistakes we made. For mathematics she simply copied the correct answers on the board, from her teacher's answer sheet, and it was up to us to figure out how to arrive at those solutions. That was the extent of her "tutoring." In all my years of schooling and teaching, I never found any teacher whose job required so little effort. And, I thought indignantly, Mama was paying a good sum for this non-education!

Cambridge Class was not a total loss, however. It was during this period that I fell in love for the first time. Robert Tung was a Chinese student from Hong Kong. He and his two buddies, Peter from Austria and Hendrix from Germany, made my life interesting despite the boring course of study, and they spent most weekends at my house. Mama was tolerant of this friendship despite the fact that she had previously, without my consent, engaged me to the son of a man we knew as Mr. Han.

By the late 1940s arranged marriages were already outdated. Mama's excuse for making the match was that because her health was unpredictable, in case of her sudden death, Mr. Han would continue my upbringing, using funds from my inheritance. Mr. Han at that time was courting Mama, whom he regarded as a desirable rich widow.

Mama lived her life during those changing times trying to find a balance between conflicting beliefs. One was that she should be an independent woman, and another was that she should continue to exert her authority over her daughters. When I protested against this unwanted engagement, Mama went into one of her hysterical breakdowns and seemed to be on the verge of death. Would I want to be burdened with the guilt of causing my mother's death? Of course I wouldn't. When I acquiesced to her demand, a quiet distance opened between us. I avoided her company and became a recluse in my own home.

At the beginning of 1947, World War II had ended and new teachers came to the school. Mere Rene Noel, our French teacher, a native French speaker from Paris, was one of them. Freshly out of the Novitiate in Paris, she was young and vivacious, and even those students who already had eight years of French had trouble with her rapid-fire speech. Mere Rene Noel soon came up with a plan to overcome this problem. She formed a French Club, "L'Etoile du Matin," and organized excursions. The nuns had a retreat house outside of town in Lao Shan, and she took us there for weekends during which the one unbreakable rule was that only French must be spoken. By the end of the year, we were all proficient in French, and the speed at which she spoke was no longer a problem. Her efforts paid off when we received the results of our O level French exam. A member of the staff of the French embassy conducted the exam, which included dictation read at a normal speed. We all passed with ease.

When the spring semester began in 1948, student enrollment had dropped considerably. Robert Tung, my first love, suddenly left with his family, without telling me. I was heartbroken. The only person with whom I could share my pain was my best friend Mary Lee. But before the end of the semester, she informed me that she too would be leaving to return to Shanghai with her family.

The reason for these sudden departures from Qingdao was the relentless eastward march of Mao Tse-tung and his Red Army toward the cities on the coast. Shanghai was considered to be the escape route to Hong Kong, which was under British control.

Mama was very aware of the dangers of Communism, but she had lived through the revolution against Empress Tsing, two World Wars, the

China-Japan War, and Japanese Occupation. How could anything be worse, she thought.

I tried to ignore the signs of unrest as I continued to enjoy my life as a teenager. While I was recovering from the loss of my first love, I attended a party where I met a businessman from Hong Kong. We began to go dancing every weekend. He always came to fetch me in a taxi and returned me the same way. Mama never even met him. Since our communication had been kept to a minimum, she and I never discussed my friendship with Jimmy Wong.

Even in my self-absorbed state, I could not help seeing the increasing number of people who were sleeping on the streets. In winter many froze to death. They had fled from the West, where Mao's army had taken over. The White Nuns of Holy Ghost School operated an orphanage outside of town. Set into the wall next to the front door of the school was a drawer where people could drop off unwanted babies. By 1948 the orphanage had exceeded its capacity. There was no more room, and the drawer was nailed shut.

Chiang Kai-shek's Kuomintang government was busy planning its own escape, so the refugees were left to their own fate. Looking back, I regret not only my failure to help, but also the state of denial in which I lived. I avoided looking at all the suffering around me. It was as though I went to and from school with blinders on. I don't recall that Mama bemoaned the plight of the refugees, nor had any teachers in school helped us reflect on the situation. Perhaps people were tired of wars, or the problems were just too overwhelming to face.

Not all the refugees were poor. Among them was a group of American priests who bought a house just down the street from ours, which made it very convenient for me to attend Mass there on a daily basis. Soon I made the acquaintance of the rector, Father Fulgence Gross. He was always full of humor, and I enjoyed chatting with him after Sunday Mass.

Unbeknownst to me at the time, a plan was in the making that would change my life. My friend Father Gross was chosen to head our school's annual retreat. During one of the retreat sessions, on the subject of Vocation, Father asked, "How many of you have ever thought of becoming a priest or nun?" I was not the only one who raised a hand.

The following Sunday after mass he invited me to step into the visitors'
parlor where he got right to the point. "Let's talk about your desire to become
a nun. How long have you had this desire?"

"Ever since third grade I have wanted some day to give my life to God
wholeheartedly, just like sister George. But when I started to go to the hill for
mass, I began to feel more attracted to the Pink Sisters," I said. This was the
first time I had articulated my hidden desire, and I surprised myself. But then,
of course, you are supposed to confess everything to the priest.

Father Gross said, "You don't want to join the Pink Sisters. They do everything in German. Since you already know English, you should be part of an
English-speaking community."

"The Pink Sisters live a silent life and all Catholics have prayers in Latin.
So what difference does it make?" I countered. Ever since I was a small child, I
had enjoyed being in places of silent meditation and solitude.

"No, no, no! I know the perfect group of American Sisters for you. Why
don't you pray about it, and I'll see what I can do." He went on talking
about the American sisters. I wanted to say, "No need to do anything now.
Remember I said 'someday'." But he was already preparing to leave.

I was relieved to be leaving, too, and I promised myself I would never give
the subject another thought. Nor would I tell anyone else about my desire...
except Mary. I dutifully observed the rule that I must not interrupt my elders
when they spoke; this time my deference would get me into even deeper trouble.

When Mary left for Shanghai, I felt I had lost my best friend. She and I
shared every detail of our lives. Only she knew how I felt about my unwanted
engagement and what it was like to date a boy who always had two body
guards and then vanished suddenly. She told me about her love/hate relationship with her sister Madeleine and her problems in her new school. After
Mary moved, she and I continued to exchange our intimacies by letter. We
wrote to each other every day and sent off bulging envelopes at least once a
week.

One day as Mama handed me one of Mary's fat letters, she said, "You two
sure have a lot to tell each other." I took this opportunity to feel Mama out.
"In her last letter, Mary mentioned she is planning to apply to American
universities. What would you think if I did the same?" Mama said, "With the
Communists almost at our back door, America would offer you better education, but I don't want to think about it now."

One evening I received an unexpected phone call from Sister Eustella, the principal of St. Joseph's School. I had never spoken to Sister Eustella, and as far as I knew she knew me only as Fung Ying's youngest sister. Sister Eustella asked me to come by her office the following day. Mama was just as surprised as I was by the call, and just as curious. When I got home after meeting with Sister Eustella, Mama was waiting for an explanation.

"Remember, I told you about my friend Mary wanting to go to America for university? Sister Eustella may be able to help me get there too," I explained. Mama looked at me quizzically. Before she could formulate another question, I quickly ended the conversation by saying, "Probably nothing will happen."

Monday after school, I walked to the corner of our school, crossed the street and mounted the steps of St. Joseph School. The principal's door was open. "Come in, come in, Gloria," said Sister Eustella. I sat on a wooden chair across from her big office desk. "Father Gross spoke very highly of you." She began asking me a series of questions and seemed to be filling out a questionnaire as I answered. I tried as politely as possible to ask her the purpose of this visit. She responded somewhat impatiently. "You want to be a nun, don't you?" Then she went on talking.

I waited for a pause to let her know that my talk about becoming a nun was actually only wishful thinking. There were insurmountable problems. My mother was a Protestant and would never allow me to take that step. I couldn't tell her, a stranger, that because of Mama I was also engaged to be married. I doubt that any of my protestations had reached her ear. In the middle of a sentence of my explanation, she said, "You may go now." As I had after my "conversation" with Father Gross, I felt overwhelmed and unheeded. They seemed to have their own motives for "helping" me, and what I had to say was irrelevant.

At home and in school, my life appeared to go on as usual. Of course I did not mention my meetings with Father Gross and Sister Eustella. I was busy cramming for my Cambridge exams, and my social life continued to consume any extra time I had.

One winter evening, Sister Eustella called again. "Come see me after school tomorrow. I have good news for you." Fortunately, Mama was next door playing mahjong with Lai Yu's parents, so I did not have to tell another white lie.

As soon as I entered her office, Sister Eustella waved a paper at me saying, "You are accepted."

"To what?" I asked.

"To become a candidate of our Congregation. You must apply for your visa and passport immediately. No time is to be lost. Once the Communists take over . . . ."

"But I still have over a year of high school to finish." I didn't have time to add that Mama knew nothing about my wishing to become a nun and would never consent to it, before Sister Eustella said, "I've already spoken to Mother Elfleda. She will give you credits for the private lessons you have taken and issue a diploma. You will attend Alverno College in Milwaukee, operated by our Sisters."

My mind went blank as she continued with a series of instructions on steps to be taken immediately. Sister Eustella telephoned Sister Fides, my former piano teacher, who quickly arrived at the door to escort me from the school to a photo shop in town. I tried to enlist the help of Sister Fides in explaining to Sister Eustella about the difficulties I faced that made going to America impossible just then. She only said, "God's ways are not our ways."

Inside the shop Sister Fides combed my hair, wrapped me in a little black cape with a white collar, and put a black veil over my head. "This is for your passport picture. It's the look of a candidate in our Congregation. Did Sister Eustella tell you that you have to go to Shanghai for your visa and passport?"

"God's ways are not our ways," I kept repeating to myself during the next few days. I suspected those nuns may have bribed God to follow their ways, but maybe it really was what God intended. What I needed desperately was a way to get Mama to go along with "God's ways."

I felt as though I had been caught in a whirlwind, and the course of my life was out of my hands. As a potential "favorite," I hoped God would find a way to get me to Shanghai.

All these years later, I have come to believe that when there is a critical question hidden inside a person, answers emerge out of the void. I don't remember what triggered Fung Ying to mention her Shanghai shopping trip last winter vacation, but I used her comments as an opportunity to ask Mama if I could visit my friend Mary. She knew how much Mary and I missed each other, and after calling our relatives in Shanghai to see if they could keep an eye on me during what would be my first solo trip away from home, she reluctantly agreed.

As Mama watched me pack, I reintroduced the topic of my future education.

"Maybe Mary can give me some hints about universities in America. Bi Yuen and her husband are already there. Maybe he can inquire for me at his University of Kentucky."

"Don't rush the matter. You still have high school to finish," Mama said. She glanced out the window at the addition to our house. She had never explained its purpose to me, but I was sure I knew what it was. Now that she had finished planning and preparing for her eldest daughter's wedding, her focus was on my future. She wanted my husband and me to live close to her. When I reflect on all the conflicts Mama faced at that time, I am grateful she often chose those that would open more doors to the future for me.

Off I went to Shanghai. To negotiate my way around the city, I was grateful once again for my friend Mary. She spoke the Shanghai dialect and was well acquainted with the layout of the city. Her family's house was not far from the American Quarter, where I had to apply for my passport and visa. Each major foreign country had its own Quarter. People lined up hours before the doors of the governmental offices opened; it was like a stampede of people trying to get out of China. Each time I saw some people emerge from the office with a downcast look, I knew they had been refused, and my heart skipped a few beats. But then I thought, "It's up to God," and relaxed. After two weeks of waiting, made tolerable only by the company of my good friend, I procured the necessary documents. Mary and I celebrated in a small restaurant and wished one another happiness and a safe journey. "God willing, we will meet again in America." Sadly, two years later Mary died in Communist-occupied Shanghai.

When I returned from visiting Mary, I waited for an opening to explain my situation to Mama. Finally, trying to sound casual, I said, "Mary whetted my appetite with all the information on American universities. She persuaded me to apply for a visa and passport, just in case I could go."

"I doubt you would ever use them," Mama said, lowering her gaze and becoming pensive.

Like her, at that time I considered it an exercise in futility. By then most foreigners and many Chinese had already left Qingdao, including the American Sisters and some of the teachers from my school. Father Gross had chosen to stay and, as he said, "convert" the communists." (Years later I heard he had suffered many years in a Communist prison. When he finally did return to America, all his teeth had been knocked out and his weakened body needed major medical attention.)

When I began to inquire about passage to America, the few remaining travel agents were in the process of shutting down. Commercial transportation was no longer available. I viewed the situation with mixed feelings. On the one hand, it was too bad I had gone to all the trouble to acquire the documents, but on the other hand I would not have to leave Mama and home. So many unknowns were associated with going to America that my familiar surroundings and people felt much more desirable.

I resumed my life and dismissed the thought of leaving home. Near the end of the school term, on a beautiful Saturday in mid-May, I was to meet my Turkish friend Almira around noon, to go horseback riding. As I opened the gate, I encountered Father Gross just as he was about to press the bell.

"Say, Gloria, do you still want to go to the United States?"

"How, Father? I haven't learned how to fly yet, and I can't swim across the Pacific Ocean." I soon noticed he was not in his usual jocular mood.

"This is serious. We can't waste time. The U.S. Marine hospital ship is leaving with the last of their personnel. I know the person in charge. If you want to go, be at the Tai Pei Pier by 1:15 sharp. That's an hour from now." He left in a hurry.

I ran back to the house and dashed up two flights of stairs. Mama asked me what I had forgotten for riding. When I caught my breath, my brain was racing as I tried to find the right words. I simply blurted, "Mama, I have a chance to go to the United States for college." I quickly told her Father Gross's offer. "Should I go?" Time seemed to stop, although only a few seconds had passed, during which my entire future was pending. Mama said, "You pack your suitcase. I'll get some cash."

I suddenly realized I had never given any thought to what nuns needed. But I did remember something from Sister Fides. Before she left for America, she handed me a little bundle saying, "Remember what you wore for the passport picture? Here's the rest of the uniform. In case you get a chance to go to America, wear this on the way." At that time, I had not even fully opened the bundle, believing I would never need it. Now I pulled it from the bottom of my dresser and checked to see if my passport and visa were still in it. I folded a summer dress and put it on top of the bundle and grabbed some underwear and socks. Mama gave me a green travel blanket and counted out nine U.S. $100 bills. "Your Big Aunt told me over the phone she and Big Uncle will meet us at the pier and bring you $100."

Years later, when I reflected on all the miracles that brought me to America at that critical moment, it struck me that if Mama did not have those U.S. dollars on hand, I could not have left. At that time, when Kuomintang currency was rapidly deflating, and people had to carry a whole sack of money even to purchase a sack of flour, Mama had the foresight to save money in a more stable currency. Or did she have an intuition that it might serve an urgent need?

Father Gross expedited my authorization to leave on the U.S. Marine ship, and at 1:00 p.m. my family and I stood on the designated pier. I wore a sky-blue cotton dress with large white dots and a light blue woolen coat. Mama clutched my arm while facing Fung Ying and Lai Yu, Big Aunt, and Big Uncle. We exchanged few words, although our hearts were full. Tear-filled eyes looked from me to the ship. My own heart was filled with a blend of pain, fear, and excitement. I was leaving everyone I loved and heading into the unknown, but I was heading for a new life in a country that was not at war. A sailor helped me into a rowboat, and I was off to my new life. Mama dropped her hankie into the boat for me. That was the last time I saw my beloved mother.

Off to America

ONBOARD THE SHIP I kept waving to my family from the railing until they were out of sight and the pier itself was just a line on the horizon. The realization of Mama's sacrifices on my behalf suddenly struck me like a blow. I stood a long while on the deck, my face and hair wet from the combination of ocean spray and tears, and I had to wring out Mama's hanky. At last I turned from the railing and went inside to face my solitary journey among strangers on this huge ship.

I was not among strangers for long, however. I spotted a group of nuns wearing the same garb as those of the Holy Ghost School. Although I recognized none of their faces, I introduced myself as a student from their school

Tai Pei Pier

Leaving for America

and mentioned the names of my teachers. They welcomed me as one of their own, and I felt secure in their company.

I could have spent the rest of my sailing time with those motherly nuns, but my teenage curiosity made me want to explore everything the ship had to offer. I roamed around and before long found myself standing and waiting for a turn to play shuffleboard. It was there that I became acquainted with Irmgard, a blond German girl a few years my senior, and Tony, a Chinese boy about my age.

In the company of my new friends, time passed quickly. On the second day of our voyage the captain announced we would make two stops, one in Nagasaki and another in Hong Kong. From Hong Kong only U.S. citizens would be allowed to continue on to America. This directive had not been made clear, and suddenly I had yet another obstacle in my course. Tony was headed to Hong Kong, and he was almost certain his parents would accommodate us while we waited for our passage to the United States. The White Nuns I had met when I first boarded the ship also said we could stay at the convent. I understood that people do open their hearts and homes during times of crisis.

On May 25, 1949, the ship docked at the Port of Hong Kong. As I left the ship I saw newsboys waving papers whose headlines announced: "Tsingtao (Qingdao) Taken Peacefully!" If I had not left when I did, I would not have been able to get out. "How wonderful are God's ways!" I exclaimed.

Irmgard and I soon found ourselves among thousands of refugees in transit to America or England. Every day we went from one travel agency to another, only to be told all seats on planes or ships headed for America were booked up until September. We doubted we could survive three more months in the subtropical heat. I had almost stopped eating, and Irmgard had developed asthma. Even more significant was the fact that she was running out of money. At last one travel agent told us there had been a cancellation for a third-class ticket aboard a ship headed for San Francisco. Because of Irmgard's asthma, we decided she should take that ticket.

With Irmgard gone, I had no one to share my frustration. In my lowest moments I felt like taking the next slow boat back to Qingdao. "Just one more day," I would say to myself. Somehow, in a mysterious way, I kept tapping into a hidden source of courage.

A few days after Irmgard's departure, I found a small travel agency in a dimly lit lane. I made my usual inquiry and the agent asked the usual questions as he flipped through his reservation book. "If you are traveling alone," he said, "a company has just booked passage on a plane for families of their employees. It's going to Seattle. There is one seat left at the rear of the plane. It will depart in three days."

"I'll take it! I'll take that seat! Is Seattle near Milwaukee, Wisconsin?" I shouted.

"No, but I can find a connecting flight for you."

I counted out $365 U.S. for a ticket on a Pan American flight bound for Seattle, Washington, a place I'd never heard of. It was in America, though, and that was good enough for me.

The plane took off at dawn on a Friday, June 15, 1949. The flying time to Seattle was supposed to be 36 hours, with a refueling stop in Anchorage, Alaska. Just before we landed in Anchorage, the Captain announced, "We have a problem with an engine. All passengers must get off the plane and remain in the waiting area." Mid-June in Alaska is not warm. We had left steaming hot Hong Kong and were now shivering in Alaska's chill. As I wrapped myself in the travel blanket Mama had given me, I was once again grateful for her forethought and her love. Since the repairs took longer than anticipated, the airline put us up overnight in a motel and provided us with food. The only food available was hamburgers. Thinking it was still Friday, I faced a moral dilemma. As a Catholic, I knew eating meat was forbidden, and if I did so I would be committing a mortal sin. If the plane crashed I would go to hell. On the other hand, I was very hungry. After I ordered a hamburger, I was relieved to learn we had gained 17 hours since leaving Hong Kong, and it was now Saturday. (Years later, when in 1963 Pope John XXIII declared freedom of conscience as the highest law, I cheered. I had always instinctively known it was true, and I thought it was a shame that Catholics needed a Pope to tell them what every human heart already knows.)

When we landed in Seattle the following day, there was of course no one at the airport to meet me. Alaska was not yet a State in 1949, so Seattle was my port of entry. I waited in a long line before an immigration officer examined my papers, only to have him stamp my visa with the words "Questionable Immigrant" and direct me to step aside and wait. "Will I be sent back?" was my immediate thought. The words of Psalm 23 came to mind, "The Lord is my shepherd. I shall not want." That helped but did not slow my rapidly beating heart. Other "questionable immigrants" were in line with me. A man led us to a van and drove us to a separate building, where a guard stood in front of an iron-barred detention room door while another guard kept watch inside.

As we were served a strange lunch of gruel and pickles, I remembered Mama's words, "God gave you a mouth. Use it to ask for help when you need it." I asked the guard if I might speak to the immigration officer, but he ordered me to go and sit down. I sat and stared at my unappetizing lunch for a while, and then more advice from Mama came to me. "Don't accept 'no' easily." This time I crafted my request and polished my English, "Excuse me for bothering you again, Sir. If you could get me a five-minute appointment with the immigration officer, I am quite certain that I can clear up the questions about my documents." He looked at me questioningly, and I thought I saw his eyes soften. He left. After a little while he returned, saying, "Be ready for your appointment in an hour."

I searched my brain for more words of wisdom. "Wear your uniform on the way," Sister Fides had instructed me. I figured I was on the way to speak with an officer who would decide my fate, so this would be the time to wear the uniform. The uniform pieces had been in my closet for nearly a year and were badly wrinkled. Nevertheless, I donned the black pleated skirt, the shirt, and the veil with the attached white collar. I put them on as best I could figure them out, and, ignoring the curious looks of my fellow detainees, I looked straight ahead and followed the guard out the door.

The immigration officer's raised eyebrows and incredulous stare reflected the strange spectacle I must have been, but I had my speech ready. "Thank you for giving me this opportunity to explain my apparel and clarify some apparent contradictions in my papers. I am on my way to become a candidate of the Sisters of St. Francis in Milwaukee, Wisconsin. I have never seen how this uniform is worn, because all the sisters in China wore the full habit. I can explain the different dates of my birthday on different documents. Some indicate my birthday according to the Chinese calendar and some reflect the Western calendar. Some of my supporting documents use my American name and the governmental papers use my Chinese name. Are there other unclear areas, Sir?" He flipped through the papers while I silently prayed. At last he raised his head, looked at my outfit, and the corners of his mouth turned up into a slight smile. "Will you raise your right hand and swear that everything you have just told me is the truth and nothing but the truth, so help you, God?"

"I do swear it is the truth."

"You have missed your flight to Milwaukee, but don't worry. I'll have my secretary get you on the next flight out."

I waited outside his office until the officer came out and said, "Let's go get your bag. Your plane is boarding." He drove me to the departure gate himself, got out of his car, and carried my suitcase. He wanted to make sure that my change of flight was not a problem. "Will someone be meeting you at the other end?" I had made no arrangement to be met at the end of this long and often-interrupted journey. I knew I should call St. Joseph Convent, but I had no coins. The officer reached into his pocket, gave me a handful of coins, and waited until the call was completed. I couldn't find words to thank him. I shook his hand and looked into his eyes while tears ran down my cheeks. I said, "Thank you. I will not forget your kindness." (Years later, as an American citizen, whenever I see news clips of immigrants waiting to be questioned by an immigration officer, I recall the kindness shown to me in Seattle and pray that such kindness be extended to them.)

In Chicago I transferred to a smaller plane and went on to Milwaukee. No one was there to meet me. (I later learned they had thought I would arrive in Chicago, and Sisters were waiting for me there.) "Well," I told myself, "so many 'angels' have been sent to me along the way, the least I can do is get myself to my final destination." I managed to find a cab and told the driver to take me to St. Joseph's Convent.

St. Joseph's Convent

I ALMOST RAN up the two flights of stone steps to St. Joseph's Convent. A Sister opened the heavy oak door. "Hello, Sister. I am Gloria Chou. I have just come from China." She pointed to the right, "This is the priest's entrance. Go to the other entrance. I'll call to the main office." I dragged my suitcase down those steps and up two more flights to the "proper" entrance. The door was already open. There stood Sister George, Sister Adolph (the other Chinese Sister from Qingdao), the Reverend Mother Eustella, and another Sister my height. Their warm smiles were mixed with laughter. I would not have passed for uniform check. The short Sister introduced herself as Sister Viola. She knew just what I needed: food, a bath, and a bed. When I finally woke up, someone was there to dress me properly, in a clean uniform set with no wrinkles.

I had just missed being inducted with one class of novices and had to wait for the next class. Sister Viola saw to it that my time would not be wasted, however. She determined I would teach English to the four other girls in my class, all of whom were from Honduras. I wanted to say "Me?! I've just come from China!" But of course I just answered, "Yes, Sister."

During my first few days of becoming orientated to the St. Joseph Convent, I walked miles of corridors, staircases, tunnels, and chapel aisles with my four Honduran companions. In the kitchen, which produced three nutritious meals a day, we met Sister Almarita, the supervisior. The kettles used to cook potatoes, rice, or oatmeal were the size of beer barrels. When I was a Novice on kitchen duty, washing dishes included scrubbing those kettles. When Sister Almarita saw me trying to reach the bottom of a kettle with a scrub brush, she pulled me from the edge, doubling up with laughter. "You could drown in there and we'd have to haul you out!"

After a week of living like a tiny fish in an ocean of strangers, unusual customs, and weird nooks and crannies, I was once again told to pack up. A bus transported me, along with my four companions from Honduras, Sister Viola, several other Sisters, and many more girls wearing the same uniform., to Aurora, Illinois, where we were to attend summer school. The new girls had all been summer school students before. Sister Viola introduced them to me as Aspirants—girls who joined after eighth grade and by going to summer school were able to complete high school in three years. About 60 of these Aspirants were in their last year of high school and would become Postulants in September. They would be entering a year-long trial period before being received into the Novitiate.

When the van approached Madonna High School, I thought I was dreaming. The building was an exact replica of St. Joseph Middle School in Qingdao! My mind flashed back to the scene of the Japanese military truck hauling our American Sisters to camp. I later learned the same blueprints had been used to construct both schools.

Madonna High School was an all-girl school staffed by our Sisters during the school year. During the summer holidays the occupants were Aspirants and teaching Sisters. In the summer of 1949, there were more than 200 students. Cots were set up in the gym, next to which were toilets and showers for athletes during the school year. A big dining room and a kitchen served as our eating area. In addition to the teaching Sisters, a group known as house Sisters specialized in cooking and laundry duties.

Since my high school background was lacking in laboratory science, I was assigned to take two courses, one in botany and another in zoology. Each class had more students than my entire Holy Ghost School or my Cambridge Class. For the first time I actually used a microscope and three-dimensional lab equipment, not just textbook illustrations. I was fascinated by my first science courses and earned an A in each class. I enjoyed having class discussions, too, and thought I might like to be a science teacher myself. My unspoken wish was not lost to powers that be.

To Thee I Consecrate

JUNE 13, 1950, marked a milestone in my life. In 12 days I would be 19 years old, but today I would become a "Bride of Christ." At 9 a.m. in the lobby of St. Joseph Convent Chapel in Milwaukee, Wisconsin, I stood with 71 other excited girls. All of us were about the same age and were dressed in our black uniforms as Postulants (candidates in training for membership as Religious of the Order of St. Francis). Each of us wore a white waist-length veil. When organ music broke the silence it was almost possible to hear our eager

My sister Mary (Bi Yuen) witnesses me
becoming a Bride of Christ.

heartbeats as the procession began to enter the beautiful Gothic chapel.

My sister Mary (Bi Yuen), her husband John, and their eight-month-old daughter Christine were sitting in one of the pews. They had driven up from their home in Lexington, Kentucky, to witness this momentous occasion. When the last girl was inside, the organ and the choir stopped. After a long silence, the crystal-clear voice of a 16-year-old Aspirant filled the chapel. As she sang "To Thee I Consecrate," my body tingled from head to toe. A sense of the sacred filled my heart, and I wanted to shout, "Yes! Yes!"

We filed to the altar railing, and Father Klink handed each girl a pack of religious garments. As he did so, he raised his voice and proclaimed, "Your name in Religion will be . . ." and pronounced the name each girl would assume from that time onward. My name was Sister Mary Grace, a name I had not chosen. Most of the girls had asked to be given the name of their grand-mother, a favorite aunt, or that of a particular saint. Since none of my older relatives had English names, I was given the name of my two sisters.

After everyone had returned to the pews, we filed out of the chapel to be invested in our religious habits and white veils. Sister Marie Patrice was happy to have a seventh sister from China. She snipped off my long dark hair into a crew-cut and wrapped my head in a white cap with a tight strap that allowed only my face to show. The habit was ankle-length, with wide wrist-length sleeves. A large rosary hung from a white rope around my waist.

Everyone stood as we re-entered the chapel as Brides of Christ. The sol-emn high mass that followed ended with a thunderous hymn of thanksgiving, "Te Deum," sung by the choir and the congregation.

What's in a Name?

IN MY EIGHT-PLUS decades of life I have been called by many different names. As the fourth daughter born to parents who desperately wanted a son, I was initially called **Ling Dee,** which means, **"Bring a Younger Brother."**

When my parents resigned themselves to the fact that they would be the parents of daughters only, my name became **Pung Pung,** which is the name of a legendary bird.

My two older sisters had their own nickname for me, which was **Doe Ze,** meaning **"Little Pea."**

When I entered elementary school in Chongqing, having fled to that city from the Japanese with my aunt and uncle, my name was **Chou Fung Chee**, which means **"Rising Phoenix."**

One of my uncles, who had studied English, gave each of us girls an English name. My sisters were Grace and Mary. The name he gave me was **Gloria.**

During World War II, when Mama transferred me to a new school, she could not remember which name my uncle had given me. Mama only knew it was one of the "G" names. She chose **Grace.**

When my oldest sister (the real Grace) came home from attending university in Peking, she insisted that I correct that mistake. Consequently, I had to stand up in front of a school assembly and explain that from now on I was to be called Gloria.

When I became a Bride of Christ as a Religious in the Order of St. Francis, I was given the name **Sister Mary Grace.**

Now I am simply **Gloria Chou** or **Fung Chee Chou.** Your choice.

Teaching in the 1950s

AFTER MY INDUCTION as a Novice in the Order of St. Francis, I participated in more schooling designed to qualify me to become a teacher in a Catholic school.

In 1951, when I was a second-year Novice, I met Alinda, a first-year Novice who would become a lifelong friend. Initially, however, we did not exchange words, because Novices at that time were not allowed to speak to anyone outside their level.

The dean of Alverno College sent the two of us to summer school to catch up on some missing courses because the Reverend Mother wanted us to start teaching in September. I helped Alinda (or "Lindy," as I called her) pass her biology course that summer.

Two years later, when Lindy and I had both taken our temporary vows and were Junior Sisters, we were assigned to teach at Holy Redeemer School in Milwaukee, Wisconsin, she in second grade and I in first.

After another two years passed, Lindy was transferred to a school in another city. Sisters were not to "hang on" to other Sisters or have friends, for fear of lesbianism. At the time, I did not even know the word or what it meant, but no one can sever the heart connection between people.

After teaching first grade at Holy Redeemer for four years, I was transferred to teach biology at Madonna High School in Aurora, Illinois. To my surprise, Sister Alinda was on the faculty as well, as a teacher of history and French. I believe the universe (or God) has a way of bringing kindred spirits together...and sometimes separating them...for good reasons, and I continued to deviate from the Rule against maintaining friendships.

During what became known as the "Sputnik Age," I had to keep up with rapid changes in science. I applied for National Science Foundation grants to pursue science courses at St. Mary's College in Winona, Minnesota, and I earned a master of science degree in 1967. During each summer I continued to receive NSF grants, which gave me the freedom to choose elective courses offered in other cities throughout the country.

My friend Lindy, meanwhile, was chosen to pursue her studies at the Sorbonne in Paris, and we still managed to keep in touch. One of my minors was French, so I was interested in the academic wealth that Lindy was sharing.

When Lindy returned to America, she was assigned to be the director of French studies at Alverno. Instead of accepting this position, Lindy left the Order, found a teaching job at Indiana University, and met and married a student in her adult education class. Harry was a Christian Scientist. It took some time and experience, but this former nun, whose ancestors were Polish Catholics, accepted the Christian Science faith and with her husband served as a missionary for 14 years in Switzerland. Whenever she returned to America, Lindy and I reconnected. We remained constant friends until Lindy's death in 2014.

While Lindy followed her life's unpredictable course, I continued to struggle with the polarity between science and my religious beliefs. I discovered *The Human Phenomenon*, a book by Pierre Teilhard de Chardin, a French priest who lived from 1881 to 1955. The author was a paleontologist (he took part in the discovery of Peking Man), theologian, and Jesuit priest whose writings were banned by the church. The book opened my eyes and my heart, and I considered *The Human Phenomenon* to be the most important book in my life.

Vatican Council II

WHEN I WAS 10 years old, in 1942, I was baptized into the Roman Catholic Church. The reigning Pope was Pius XII. I had to study the Baltimore Catechism (which served as the standard Catholic school text from 1885 to the late 1960s), and learn the dogmas of the Catholic Church. Although no one checked my grasp of these requirements, I knew I had to abide by them and take them seriously. When I became a member of the Order of St. Francis, more rules were added to my life. In all instances, I had to accept these rules unquestioningly, by faith. "Blind obedience" was the rule by which we lived.

Why did I choose to bind myself to such rigid strictures in my life? I had read the biography of St. Theresa of Lisieux in third grade, and I wanted to be

My more comfortable habit,
post-Vatican II.

a saint just like her. St Theresa said, "I want to spend my heaven doing good on earth." That was what I wanted, at all cost.

With that background view of myself as a naïve but pious child, we move ahead nearly 20 years. I was a Sister of the Order of St. Francis when Pope Pius XII died, in October 1958, and all the Cardinals went to Rome to elect a new Pope. Every evening we watched for the announcement of a new Pope, which would be signaled by white smoke from the chimney of the Vatican building. Gray, gray, gray smoke wafted out for more than a week.

Finally, "It's white!" I shouted along with my Community. To our great surprise, when the new Pope came out to the balcony and was announced as Pope John XXIII, we learned he had not even been one of the nominees. He was Giuseppe Roncalli, Archbishop of Vienna, 78 years old. We thought it probable that, when the electors could not reach a consensus, they chose what they considered to be an old man who would soon die. In the meanwhile, they would have time to find a more suitable candidate.

How wrong they were. Within his first year, this "old" new Pope called for the Cardinals to return to Rome for the opening of Vatican Council II. (The only other such Council had been held nearly 100 years earlier.) Vatican II took place at St. Peter's Basilica in four sessions between 1962 and 1965, and the Catholic Church has never been the same since. The theme of Vatican II was reconciliation.

The Dogmas of the Church, as well as those regulating the lives of Religious men and women, were to be updated. I read everything I could get my hands on regarding the Council. Aggiornamento was my new vocabulary word for renewal. (Aggiornamento means "bringing up to date" and "a spirit of change and open-mindedness.")

On the radio I heard the Pope say, "The greatest law is freedom of conscience." ("Not blind obedience," I thought with relief.) With all that Aggiornamento was bringing about, I had never felt so alive.

What affected me most directly were the changes in Religious life. It seemed the Pope had opened a window to let fresh air into an archaic church. He made thinking permissible. With these changes, I felt like a newly sprouted seed growing toward the sun, opening and stretching. I became part of a steering committee in my Community, working to implement the Council's changes in the *Rule of Life* book. I surprised myself by leaving my usually reticent demeanor behind and becoming an articulate speaker, and I remembered with gratitude my mother's love for freedom of inquiry.

The new version of the *Rule of Life* book proclaimed, "Every Religious shall be a woman of prayer." That was all. It did not spell out pages and pages of how, what, and when she was to pray, as the old book had done.

The church was made more accessible to parishioners. Masses could be said in languages other than Latin, with priests facing the congregation. Nuns could wear civilian clothing and converse openly with their peers. For the first time, too, we were given a small amount of pocket money to call our own.

My religious Community, the Order of St. Francis (OSF), had been founded in Milwaukee, Wisconsin, while the headquarters of most other orders were in Rome. Because of our short history, we immediately began implementing the changes for women Religious. We changed our title to School Sisters of St. Francis (SSSF) because most of our members were involved in education.

We traded our black veils and the white cloth covering our hair for a soft veil over exposed hair. A two-piece dress, with a below-the-knee hem replaced floor-length garb. Soon we were able to choose gray, black, or blue as the color of our habits.

The Superior of each local Community had previously had the authority to command blind obedience. Her permission was required for some of our most trivial activities. After Vatican II we were able to elect a coordinator. The Reverend Mother had previously assigned us the places where we lived and worked. Her word was not to be challenged.

In the spirit of Vatican II, I proposed that, as professional women, each sister should be able to apply for her own job. I did not anticipate the fear that freedom would engender in some Sisters. Previously, a nun was always guaranteed a job and a place to live. Now she had to deal with such strange concepts as job searches, resumes, interviews, and rejection.

Sisters could now choose to live with one or a few other sisters instead of in a large Community. Four of us soon moved out of our 16-member Community. I interviewed and was accepted for a teaching job at Driscoll High School, north of Chicago, a school with an innovative curriculum.

Like me, many Religious and priests welcomed the changes Vatican II brought about, but it also introduced soul-searching questions that had been suppressed for many years. As a result, many individuals left their Orders. It was a time of suffering for those who left as well as for those who remained. I was among the latter group, but I had never before felt so alive.

Unfortunately, as predicted, Pope John XXIII did not live long. He died on June 3, 1963. In his four years as Pope, however, he accomplished sweeping and long-lasting changes, not only for the Roman Catholic Church, but also for the world. He laid the cornerstone for Ecumenism—conversations between Christian traditions and Jews. Unfortunately, his successor, Pope Paul VI, reverted in many ways to the old traditions.

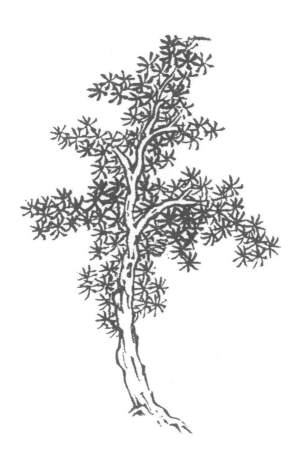

St. Mary's College . . . and George

BETWEEN 1964 AND 1967 I spent every summer in the small college town of Winona, Minnesota, pursuing a master's degree in science. The college nestled into bluffs on the banks of the Mississippi River, from which it operated a marine research center. The setting was ideal for my courses in terrestrial and aquatic ecology.

In 1964 I still wore the long black habit and soft veil of my order, so it was quite a struggle for me to climb up and down hills and over slippery rocks to conduct research in terrestrial ecology. The men in the class seemed hesitant to grab the hand or arm of a nun, although one, a man named George, did stay close enough to me to help in case I fell.

After four weeks, we moved on to aquatic ecology and were divided into teams of four to a boat. I was the only woman on my team, and George did not hesitate to help me into and out of the boat assigned to our team. Thus began our curious friendship.

Often, while we waited for our teammates to arrive after lunch, George would bombard me with questions, many of which showed how little he knew about the Catholic Church and his curiosity about nuns. He even asked me if I could get married! My response revealed my displeasure. I answered, "No! And I don't want to!"

I learned that George had grown up Jewish in a predominantly Christian neighborhood and had been treated badly as a boy. After college he married Phyllis and taught high school in New Jersey. Every evening during the St. Mary's summer sessions he talked with Phyllis on the phone, and I knew they loved one another.

As a result of the many changes brought about by Vatican II, many nuns, brothers, and priests, including some of my closest friends, were requesting dispensation from their vows. Many married. I chose to remain a Religious and delve deeper into the life I had chosen. Men, of course, were off-limits, but I was confident that George and I could have a meaningful friendship and that each of us could grow from our experiences together.

During Vatican Council II when Pope John XXIII said, "The greatest freedom is freedom of conscience," those words became etched into my mind and heart. I began to question all the mindless "beliefs" I had accepted in the past. George played devil's advocate in our talks and stirred deeper into the vessel of my belief system. Sometimes, as I tried to meet his challenges, a voice within me said, "I don't really believe this either."

During our free days, George and I drove around to see the natural sights surrounding the college. It's possible that we may have missed some of them, though, so engrossed were we in our arguments and dialog. On one of these side trips, George screeched to a halt in front of a motel, explaining, "Sister Chou, I promised a colleague I would pick him up in Chicago on my way back to the East Coast. I have to call him to make arrangements to meet," and off he dashed to use the phone.

When he returned to the car, George was laughing. He explained, "My friend started telling me about his summer. I cut him short with, 'I've got to go. I have a nun locked inside my car.' I heard my friend's phone fall to the floor. Everyone in my school knows I am a confirmed agnostic."

At the end of the summer George drove me back to Madonna Convent in Aurora, Illinois.

For the next three summers, George picked me up in Aurora on his drive north to Winona. The six-hour drive gave us ample opportunity to continue our discussion. Sometimes he got so engrossed in asking his question or rebutting my response that he gestured with both hands off the steering wheel until I shouted, "You drive; I'll do the talking."

The theme of George's questions was 'How could an intelligent woman like you allow yourself to be brainwashed with such stupid ideas? You aren't living in the real world.' Gradually, I felt I was being re-educated.

At the end of our last summer at St. Mary's, George signed up for an extra two-week course after the regular summer session. He drove me to the station to catch the Burlington train to Aurora. As we stood on the platform, with my black suitcase on the ground between us, George was silent...for a change. I thanked him for the kindness and generosity he had shown me. Still he was silent, although he strutted around me like the king in *The King and I*. When the train pulled in, I boarded and found a seat at a window. George stepped up and wrote "Good-bye" on the dusty window.

Alone in the moving train, I reflected on four summers of almost nonstop conversation in our strange relationship. An image of an empty room came to mind. Some of the wallpaper in the room had been stripped off. I felt I was that room. George had held up each of my deeply ingrained beliefs like a strip of wallpaper, asking me, "Do you still want to keep this?" Although I didn't give him the satisfaction of knowing how deeply he had penetrated into my faith, I did feel the need to give more careful consideration to my beliefs and in the future not accept any "truth" unless it corresponded with who I am and what I value.

Over the years George and I kept in contact. The last time I saw him was in 1987. I had a meeting in Princeton, and I spent two days with him and Phyllis. More recently, I called in 2012 after Super Storm Sandy had devastated the East Coast and the State of New Jersey had been declared a disaster. It was good to hear George's voice and learn that, although they had been without power for several days, he and Phyllis were unhurt and their property had suffered no major damage.

As good as he was at conversation and intellectual argument, George has been a poor correspondent. After that telephone conversation some three years ago, I have not heard from George, although I continue to hold him dear to my heart.

St. Paul University

AFTER A DECADE of classroom teaching in Illinois, I began to realize I did not want to spend the rest of my professional life as a classroom teacher. With the new horizons opened by Vatican II, I realized I wanted to work one-on-one in a counseling situation that combined psychology and spirituality.

I requested a discernment session with my Provincial, Sister Lenora. After consultation with her Council members, she sent me a letter advising me to take a year off and pray (listen) to determine the direction in which my heart's desire led and what job would be suitable. Although the term "sabbatical" was not used, it was implied. Of course, as a nun, I was expected to give service without financial compensation. I did not avail myself of that opportunity and kept searching for a suitable course.

In my search for a personal and spiritual counseling program, I was disappointed to discover the two largest Catholic Universities in Chicago did not offer that combination. If they had, I could have commuted to classes from my convent in Aurora, where I was teaching. The only school that seemed to fit my requirements was St. Paul University, in Ottawa, Canada.

I inquired about entering St. Paul's pastoral counseling program and sent my academic record. The director of the program called to inform me that my theology needed updating to encompass the many changes due to Vatican II. Fortunately, an upcoming summer session at St. Paul offered those two requirements, Christology and Ecclesiology. I would have to hurry, though, as those classes were to begin in two days.

I had been about leave to spend a week with my friend Lindy at her family's cabin on a lake in Indiana. It was another dilemma, but I could not waste this academic opportunity. True to the pattern of my life, I flew to Ottawa the very next day and spent my first night in Ottawa in a motel. (Until I consulted a map, I had no idea even where the city was, and I had no time to consult Sister Lenora about the choice I had made.)

The next morning, after attending my first lecture, I asked where the residences were. I was told there were none, and students had to find their own housing. I accepted the offer by one sister to let me stay for the summer with her in her rented apartment. After my second class, I sent Sister Lenora a telegram telling her where I had landed and adding, "Send money, details later."

I attended classes and tried to get acquainted with other students. Most of my fellow students were attending only the summer session. I met a young woman named Vicky Uy, who was from Manila. She and three other young Religious of the Sacred Heart (RSCJ) were studying for a program in Missiology, preparing to be missionaries. After the summer session, Vicky would remain for the academic year. (Unbeknownst to her, Vicky was being groomed to be the headmistress at the International School of the Sacred Heart in Tokyo, and it was necessary for her to stay for the advanced program in Missiology.)

Our Ecclesiology lecturer was Father Peelman, a young Belgian priest who spoke fluent German and French but was just learning English, the language in which he was to lecture. He was a brilliant man, but his lectures often left us with many questions. As a result, we students always queried Father Peelman at our coffee breaks.

At one such gathering, Father Peelman said to me, "I saw you coming out of a house on Nelson St. Do you live there? If so, how do you get to the University?"

"I take two different buses," I replied. "It takes about 40 minutes."

"I have someone drive me to the university from only a few houses south of yours. Would you like a ride?"

And so it was decided. From that point on, my roommate and I rode to school with Father Peelman in a car driven by Father Jacques L'Heureux, the university's vice-rector for financial affairs. When I learned he was a vice-president at St. Paul, I nearly shouted at him, asking "What kind of university is this that does not have student housing? Vicky Uy and I have been offered scholarships for the upcoming academic year, she at St. Louis University and I at San Francisco University. If we cannot find a suitable place here, we will go to those schools."

Soon after, at another coffee break, I felt a tap on my shoulder, "You got your checkbook?" It was Father L'Heureux. He had discussed our dilemma with the priest who administered Deschatelet, a residence for priests and seminarians, who agreed to open the third floor to Religious women. The residence was right next to St. Paul. Vicky grabbed her checkbook, and we signed up for two apartments. Our apartment hunting was concluded. We would be next-door neighbors and students during the upcoming year. What we didn't know yet, however, was how important our friendship would be. Nor did I realize how important a role Jacques L'Heureux would play in my life.

Jacques

FATHER JACQUES L'HEUREUX took a special interest in Vicky and me and the three Asian companions from her order. Throughout the year, he hosted us on excursions to a cottage his Community owned. While staying at the cottage, we were introduced to ice fishing, attended a maple syrup festival, and experienced several other unique Canadian celebrations.

At the completion of my pastoral counseling program and the end of the academic year on May 1, I stopped by Fr. L'Heureux's office to thank him for his kindness and hospitality throughout the year. When he learned I was leaving the following day, and that my friends and I had already made plans for the evening, he invited me to have lunch with him the next day, before I left Ottawa.

Jacques L'Heureux, my Soul Mate.

The following noon, Jacques and I drove to a cozy family restaurant in Hull, a town near Ottawa, where the wine and conversation flowed and we savored the Quebecois cuisine. Our talk turned to Teilhard de Chardin and our words flew back and forth across the table. I had discovered de Chardin several years earlier as I struggled with the conflicts between science and religion. I knew at the time how important de Chardin's *The Human Phenomenon* was in my life. Now, several years later, that French priest's philosophy became a pivotal influence in the uniting of our two minds and hearts. As we lingered over lunch, our eyes met, our hearts fluttered, and as Jacques later put it, "we flipped" for each other. On what I have come to consider "the miracle of May 2, 1974," we two celibates formed a loving bond that lasted 40 years, until Jacques' death in July, 2014.

At the time our friendship began, Jacques and I each had a close friend of the opposite sex. Jacques' friend was Francoise, a married mother of seven children. My friend was Frank, an ordained priest. We knew the boundaries of our commitments in regard to these individuals; we also knew, however, that the bond between the two of us was something entirely different.

In the 40 years of our friendship, Jacques and I reunited numerous times. During the years when I was working in Tokyo, I returned to the United States and Canada for my summer vacations, and Jacques and I always got together on those occasions. In the summer of 1993, my last summer in Japan, I decided to remain to see as much of that country as I could, as I sensed I would not return. Staying in Japan, however, meant I would not see Jacques for an entire year.

Knowing of the importance of our relationship, Jacques' friend Francoise paid for him to travel to Japan to visit me. After a few days in Tokyo, we flew to Qingdao, the city of my birth, where we met my sister Fung Ying. Under the Communist government she and her husband Lai Yu and their family were all forced to live in a very small apartment. From Qingdao, Fung Ying took Jacques and me to several major places of interest. Jacques was fascinated by China's antiquities.

Prior to our travels in Japan and China, Jacques and I had visited his family in Maniwukee, a small village north of Ottawa. There I met his mother and father. His father had owned a general store since Jacques was a boy, and Jacques had helped his father in the store while his mother cared for Jacques' nine younger siblings.

Looking back, I believe at least four factors contributed to the depth and length of my relationship with Jacques. Those factors include communication (we were both good correspondents through letters, visits, phone calls, and email), common interests (books, physical activities, art, and music), beliefs and values, and shared friends and associates.

In 1999, Jacques gathered all the letters we had exchanged on our yearly May 2 anniversaries, photocopied them and placed them in a handmade-paper folder, which he presented to me on our May 2 anniversary visit. After Jacques died, I received two large boxes in the mail, each containing cards we had exchanged.

Jacques was my soul mate. We read together *Love is Stronger than Death*, a book by Cynthia Bourgeault. The author, a married Episcopal priest and mother, tells of her relationship with a monk, Brother Rabe. They believed two soul mates could help one another grow even after death.

While I grieved the loss of my soul's mate, I wrote the following poem:

Loss of a loved one left a hole in my heart.
Grief follows attachment to his form.
When form is gone
Spirit is clearer and nearer,
Sharpening the reality of existential impermanence
Infinite possibilities for our spirits to grow
Separately and together.
Freedom to go beyond the border of exclusivity
Had been the precious pearl in our love.

Discovering What Really Matters

FOLLOWING THE ACADEMIC year I spent at St. Paul University in Ottawa (1973-74) pursuing a master's degree in pastoral counseling, I was no longer a student and once again without a job. During that academically demanding year, I had been too busy to ask myself the question, "If I am not going to be a classroom teacher, then what should I do?" My religious community expected me to find myself a job. (I almost regretted that it was I who had proposed that as professional women we should be able to compete for jobs with our lay peers.)

I didn't have to endure that state of anxiety for long. I received a letter from my former principal in Aurora, Illinois, offering me a job for the 1974-75 academic year. Best of all, I was to teach one religion class and serve as a personal counselor to students. I could not have made a better plan; I was overwhelmed with gratitude.

Although I enjoyed my new role and my new responsibilities, I once again grew to be dissatisfied. Something was brewing inside me. It was not giving up teaching that I wanted; I was ready for more mature interactions.

Once again, before I could become too concerned about my need to have a job, an offer came. St. Mary's College was undertaking its Aggiornamento, or renewal. The president of the college had agreed to replace the institution's single chaplain with a campus ministry team, and I was invited to be the lone woman on the team. (The others were four priests and one Christian Brother.) St. Mary's College was a Christian Brothers institution, and its president, Brother George, an outstanding nuclear scientist, was on the faculty of the biology department. I had audited a class Brother George taught while I was studying for my master of science degree at St. Mary's. The offer to join the campus ministry team seemed like a dream come true. It was at St. Mary's where I had spent four invigorating and happy summers. I loved the environment there, the opportunities for lifelong learning experiences, and the emphasis on outdoor activities.

None of the five members of the newly created team had any past experience with campus ministry, and we had to create our own job descriptions and activities. I rejected the suggestion that I serve as the group's secretary, as I didn't want to fall into a gender-specific stereotype. I insisted that my responsibilities allow me to be present to students in their various situations. I lived in a suite in a women's dorm. A male faculty member lived upstairs with the male students. Although we had no disciplinary duties, the administration wanted an adult presence in each dorm to be available for personal contact with the students.

As we worked together, I realized I had much more in common with Brother Jim Fournier than with the three priests on the team. The priests seemed much more concerned with Catholic Church dogma and protocol than with what Brother Jim and I felt was our responsibility to the students. (A few years later, a year before I left my life as a Religious, Jim left the brotherhood. He subsequently married, and he and his wife and I have remained friends throughout the years.)

We campus ministry team members had weekly meetings, at which our views went in diverging directions. The priests wanted to impose strictures that Brother Jim and I thought didn't fit with campus ministry. For example, they often complained that too few students attended mass, and we thought church attendance irrelevant to our work.

I had a friend in the psychology department, whom I invited to come and observe a meeting to see if the five of us could get past some of our differences. After he attended that meeting, he told me he believed some members of the team had hidden agendas and were trying to push those agendas without using the language. He suggested that we replace one meeting a month by going out to lunch. As soon as we adopted this suggestion, the more relaxed atmosphere smoothed things out. It was another way of counseling. All of the members wanted to be known as individuals and to have their egos stroked.

Since I was not an ordained minister, I had no Sunday responsibilities, and I began to spend most of those free days up in the hills surrounding the campus. At first I took along a book to read, but I soon discovered I never did any reading. I just sat on a rock and took in the beauty that surrounded me. Far below was the Mississippi River, with Wisconsin to the east and Iowa to the south. Several times, in the stillness of nature or in the song of a bird, I received a silent but persistent message: "Only one thing is necessary. Love God with your whole heart and soul, and love your neighbor as yourself." The call to a contemplative life, which I had experienced as a child, reemerged. By 1979 I realized I was once again approaching a bend in the path of my life journey.

Still Point, 1979

"WHAT REALLY MATTERS?" I kept asking myself this question during quiet moments. As I sat on a hillside in Minnesota in silent contemplation, a memory from my youth floated clearly to the surface of my mind, the vision of the silent procession of the Pink Sisters. I took the image to be an answer, or at least a hint at an answer.

Not long after that, our campus ministry team attended an ecumenical conference in Boulder, Colorado. Each major Religious tradition had a leader. Ours was Brother David Steindl-Rast, a Benedictine monk from California. With the exception of a few speaking engagements, he lived as a contemplative throughout the year.

At the conference I requested and was granted a consultation with Brother David. I shared my intuition that I was about to move away from an active life of service, but I didn't know what direction my life should take. I only knew I wanted to live more as a Mary than a Martha. As a nun, I was supposed to be women of prayer, but I was always busy about more "time-urgent" matters. Even though I had made a vow of poverty, I lacked nothing. I loved the rituals of the Roman Catholic Church but I was strongly attracted to Eastern spirituality.

Brother David recommended that I look into Still Point House of Prayer and maybe make a retreat there. I made my typical quick decision to follow his advice.

In the summer of 1979 I flew to Still Water, New York, in the foothills of the Adirondack Mountains, for a 30-day retreat. A bus took me to a farmhouse nestled in the middle of 80 acres of trees, where I met the four members of the community, two Religious and two laywomen. (Still Point was open to receive men and women of any faith.)

After an orientation conversation, I was directed to a hermitage further into the forest, where I found a small cottage with rustic beauty. It had a homemade table and chair, and a throw rug in front of a cot. I was relieved to find the cottage had an indoor toilet and sink, as I have an aversion to outhouses. This tiny cabin was to be my home for 30 days. Time for prayer and contemplation? I might have more time than I had wished for.

At night, as I stood outside before I went to sleep, my pulse synchronized with the twinkling stars. In that deep silence I listened to the sounds of the wild. During the day, I observed the birds, chipmunks, and other animals, which, along with the sight and fragrance of the wildflowers, gave me a glimpse into the abundance in God's creation. The sounds and smells of the wild even followed me indoors. One night I woke up feeling spider webs on my face, and tiny spiders covered my bed. Welcome to wilderness, I thought.

During those 30 days, the only human contact I had was a daily meeting with Sister Sylvia, Still Point's spiritual director and founder. Whatever I learned about the community I learned from her. Other than those brief daily interruptions, I was surrounded by non-human companions, in the midst of an immense but indescribable Presence.

Before I left, I learned I could become a guest member of Still Point for one year.

Back at St. Mary's College in Winona, Minnesota, as I resumed my campus ministry activities, I prayed for guidance during the next few months. Before the end of the year, I decided to resign my job. I also requested dispensation from my vows as a School Sister of St. Francis. (If I became a member of Still Point, I would not be able to keep in touch with the SSSF due to distance and a lack of money.) Still Point members lived simply, but without a vow of poverty. They were vegetarians, and a big vegetable garden provided the majority of their food. In addition, neighbors who were invited to dinner often brought boxes of fruit to augment the Still Point members' diet.

Members also worked in the surrounding community. For four hours twice a week each member worked as a domestic helper for pay. We had a waiting list of "customers" for our services, as we were dependable and scrupulously honest workers.

We residents also took turns cooking. When it was my turn, I always searched the cupboards for high-protein foods like wheat germ, to add to the bread I enjoyed making. One time my friend Jacques came to visit me at Still Point, bringing with him one large bucket of peanut butter and another of honey. These were welcome gifts indeed.

By deciding to spend a year at Still Point, I took two more major turns in my life journey. In retrospect, I don't believe I had any fear regarding my uncertain future. I had gained confidence in Divine Guidance, which had never failed me in the past. I believed, and continue to believe, that wherever I am, God is.

Family Reunion in Qingdao

AFTER I LEFT Still Point and my life as a School Sister of St. Francis, I spent time visiting my friend Jacques in Ottawa and traveling to Colorado to see my sister Mary (Bi Yuen). Mary and I decided we would return to Qingdao for a family reunion with our older sister Fung Ying (Grace), who had remained in China with her husband and moved in with Mama to care for her until her death.

Soon after the couple had moved into Mama's apartment, the government forced the family to move into smaller and smaller quarters, until all eight people were living in a single room. Everyone in the building cooked on a small kerosene stove in the hallway. There was one shared toilet on each floor of the building. When Chairman Deng Xiaoping replaced Chairman Mao Tse-tung, living conditions for the people gradually improved. My sister and her family were assigned to an apartment with three small bedrooms, a tiny kitchen, and a toilet compartment. (Bathtubs were considered bourgeois. The government had bathtubs torn out from private quarters and built public bath houses. I could only imagine how Mama must have missed her daily hot bath.) She died in 1967, during the first year of the Cultural Revolution, which lasted from 1966 to 1976. (The Cultural Revolution occurred as Mao felt he was losing power. He gathered around him a vigilante band of uneducated youths and directed them to eradicate the bourgeoisie in China by destroying works of art and culture and Western influences and denouncing intellectuals and their pursuits.)

I flew to Beijing in June of 1981, exactly 32 years after I had left Qingdao for America. My sister Mary and her husband John flew separately from Denver with a tour group they had organized. I had prepared for my visit by strengthening my Chinese language skills, acquainting myself with the current political situation in China, and saving money. Fung Ying had sent me a list of things she wanted me to bring to her in China. The list included a color television set and a name-brand camera. As a recently laicized nun, having left the School Sisters of St. Francis only a year earlier, I owned neither of these items myself; nor did I have any extra money.

From Beijing it was a seven-hour train ride to Qingdao, where Fung Ying, her husband Lai Yu, and their son and daughter-in-law ran to me as I descended from the train. Tears flowed as we greeted one another. My sister kept looking at me incredulously, finding it hard to believe her little sister had returned after so many years. I remembered the last time I had seen her, when the family waited with me on the pier before I was to board a U.S. Navy ship destined for America in 1949.

Fung Ying and Lai Yu welcomed me into their humble apartment, where I slept in Mama's bed and cried myself to sleep missing her. Mary and John and their tour group were staying in a Western-style hotel in Qingdao.

Because Fung Ying was a member of the City Council, we were given a welcome-home dinner. A limousine picked us up—a rare privilege. Waiters in white uniforms served us. Other Council members were also present at this dinner We were greeted like celebrities, because we were the first overseas Chinese to return to Qingdao for a visit, and also because my sister was a prominent personage.

Fung Ying herself hosted another dinner to which she invited a number of family members, both close and distantly related. I later learned the cost of that dinner was about 100 yuen, equal to one month of Fung Ying's salary. (Her salary was above that of an ordinary worker, who earned about 35 yuen a month.)

Together Fung Ying and I visited many places I remembered from my youth. We were not able to go inside my schools, St. Michael's Cathedral, or the Protestant church my family had attended. The one place I really wanted to see was our home on Roen Chung Road. Fung Ying got permission for that visit, but not before she had presented the authorities with expensive gifts.

Before the Communists "liberated" Qingdao in 1949, my family had lived comfortably in a residential area in a three-story red brick house. By 1981 the area where we had lived had been re-zoned for multiple housing and was designated as a hostel for out-of-town Chinese visitors. In keeping with socialist policies, the government required every visitor to register at the Housing Bureau. Visitors who did not have relatives or friends in the city were assigned to a hostel such as our home had become. My sister told me that practice was a means of total social control.

As the taxi approached our house, I noticed the concrete wall that surrounded it, which was topped by iron spikes interwoven with chicken wire. Until that moment, I had never realized these forbidding spikes were meant to keep out the poor. I felt a pain in my chest as I thought, "This is wrong; my parents were supposed to be devout Christians."

The comfortable home of my childhood had undergone many changes. Where the flower, fruit, and vegetable gardens had been was now just an expanse of compacted mud. The pond was dried up, the dilapidated arbor was no longer capable of supporting wisteria, and the moon-viewing pavilion had fallen to ruin. The wheels of roller skates would have sunk into potholes along the walkway.

Inside the house, we saw that every room contained two or three cots, each with a chair beside it. A long wooden stand held an equal number of basins and water pitchers. Even the bathroom had become a small bedroom. There was no bathtub (bourgeois!) or commode. Instead, a squat toilet and sink had been installed in our former broom closet.

I wondered what had happened to our many pieces of beautifully carved furniture. Earlier in the week when we walked around the city, my sister and I had stopped at a Friendship Store. There we saw antique furniture, vases, and scrolls similar to those that used to fill our home. These items could now be purchased only with foreign currency.

At the end of the tour of our former home, I mentally calculated it now provided sleeping places for 50 people. When I left home in 1949 only four people remained in the home—my mother, an adopted brother, and two domestic helpers. As the gates closed behind us, we were too saddened to speak. Furthermore, it was not advisable that we express our feelings within hearing of the taxi driver.

When we returned to Fung Ying's apartment, she said, "Before she died, Mama requested that your name replace hers on the deed to the house. Of course it's only a formality, and the paper is registered in the Bureau of Administration for Housing, but the government is beginning to return properties to foreign owners, just to save face. You are a U.S. citizen. If you designate me as your manager, we could request to have the house returned to you."

My sister, her husband, their son and his wife, and the couple's four-year-old son were currently living in a two-bedroom apartment. Fung Ying told me that her number two daughter, Mimi, had been ordered to work in a country district during the Cultural Revolution. That daughter and her husband could return to Qingdao only if she had a legal place to live. Every habitable space in the city was occupied in 1981. I saw long lines of people outside the Housing Bureau building waiting for permission to return to Qingdao. The possibility of bringing Mimi back provided me with a reason to inquire about the possibility of repossessing "my" home. (Later, after seven years of persistent effort, Fung Ying received a small sum of money from the government. With that money we got permission to buy an apartment, where Mimi and her husband and daughter have lived since 1989.

Before I left to return to the United States, I thanked Fung Ying and Lai Yu for taking care of Mama all the years until she died. I said, "What can I do for you?" They simultaneously stated, "We want to go to America." I promised to do what I could. (Mary and John had recently sponsored their son to move from China to America. When the young parents had left China many years earlier, pressure from the baby's paternal grandparents had forced them to leave their infant son behind.)

Looking back on that return visit to China, I thought about the contrast between the poverty imposed on the Chinese people by the Communist government and my acceptance of the vow of poverty when I became a nun. There was a choice with a higher purpose in the latter, none in the former.

I was also inspired by my sister's spirit as a survivor. A self-taught dietitian, she had been director of therapeutic nutrition in the municipal hospital, a position second in importance only to that of the hospital director. The Communist government had singled her out and made her life almost unbearable because she was a college graduate who had grown up as a capitalist in Christian family. From her high-ranking position she was demoted to the lowly job of cleaning the hospital's toilets at the end of her long workday. In spite of this treatment, she strove to build on her knowledge of home economics and continued to study therapeutic dietary practices. In addition to her hospital service, she started a school to teach nutrition to nurses, and she also taught infant and senior nutrition on national television.

My brother-in-law, too, suffered under the communists. A former concertmaster in a university orchestra, he was made to watch as the Red Guards smashed his violin. Both husband and wife were compelled to attend nightly four-hour indoctrination sessions designed to convert them to the Communist ideology. These sessions were in addition to my sister's typical 14-hour workdays.

A woman called "Auntie Jing" cared for my sister's four children while Fung Ying worked her long hours. Auntie Jing, who had the bound feet of an earlier time, was a devout Catholic. Every morning before coming to the house to care for the children, she secretly attended an underground mass.

I later learned that one time the Red Guards came to the house and asked her to confess that the family's conversation included opinions opposed to the Cultural Revolution. Auntie Jing denied it. When the guards threatened to beat her, she said, "You can beat me to death. I never heard such conversation. I cannot tell a lie." (No doubt such conversations did take place in the home, but Auntie Jing, because she didn't eat with the family, was never privy to such talk, so technically, she was not telling a lie.)

Before my mother died, she expressed a wish to my sister. If ever the government returned our house, Auntie Jing should receive money for her retirement. With the money we received in 1988 in payment for our house, in addition to purchasing the apartment for my niece and her husband, we were able to ease Auntie Jing's retirement and help fulfill my mother's wish.

Blue Collar Jobs

AFTER 1980, the year when I resigned from the School Sisters of St. Francis, left Still Point House of Prayer, and visited my sister Fung Ying, I returned to America and faced another challenge. In response to a plea from Fung Ying and Lai Yu, I had vowed to do what I could to sponsor them in immigrating to the United States. Now I had to find a way to fulfill that promise.

When she learned about my promise, my sister Mary bombarded me with questions and told me what it means to sponsor someone to immigrate to America. First of all, I would need a lot of money. I had no money and no home. In fact, I had never even had a "real" paying job.

Mary and her husband John, who owned a restaurant in Longmont, near Boulder, Colorado, offered to let me work in their restaurant. They said, "You can be our waitress until you get a 'proper' job." I accepted the offer, although I knew I was supremely unqualified to be a waitress. Nuns did not even go to restaurants! At age 18 I had gone straight into a convent from my family home where servants waited on us for meals.

"Well, it will be a learning experience," I told myself, "and it will pay for a studio apartment."

I soon learned there is an art to waiting tables, especially in a good restaurant. I practiced my people skills and learned the tricks of the trade. In doing so I acquired an appreciation for waiters and waitresses.

Still, I was barely scraping by. One day I swallowed my pride and mustered the courage to go to the welfare office. The application form contained words beyond my vocabulary. "It takes a PhD to fill out this form," I thought, as I stood in line to hand in my incomplete application. When I overheard the man in front of me say he had a PhD in chemistry, I crumpled my application, dropped it in a wastebasket, and left the office.

My preference in reading material had always been inspirational books; now my daily reading was the want ads in the newspaper. Most employers preferred people who were bilingual—but in English and Spanish. Finally I spotted a job ad without that preference. There was an opening in the assembly line at Celestial Seasonings Tea Company. It was a minimum-wage job in a shift that began at 7 a.m., too early for the public bus. I had no car, but I somehow managed a down payment on a used Honda Civic.

Thus began my job as a factory worker for $3.75 an hour. Beginning at 7 a.m. I stood for eight hours a day, with an hour for lunch. As the conveyor belt passed my station, I packed tea bags into boxes. Speed was the essence of a good worker. After the first week I began to enjoy the mindless job, and knowing it was temporary gave me comfort. My thoughts floated free. I was surprised to find that occasionally having no thoughts at all was a peaceful feeling.

In an attempt to be sociable, I began to ask questions of those who worked near me on the assembly line." Is this what you plan to do the rest of your life?" I asked. One girl had dropped out of a vocational-technical school. Another had barely finished high school.

Using my experience as a guidance counselor, I tried to broaden their horizons and show them they had other possibilities. A few months later, when I was leaving yet another low-paying blue-collar job, I went back to Celestial Seasonings to get cartons to ship my belongings to my "proper job" (to use my sister's term). I learned one of the girls I had befriended had registered for college and another had gone back to voc-tech school to learn photography so she could work for a newspaper. My own horizon had already opened to include a contract that would take me overseas.

International School of the Sacred Heart

VICKY UY AND I had been friends since we were students together at St. Paul University in Ottawa during the 1973-74 school year. She had been a Religious of the Sacred Heart, and a student in Missiology, when I was a School Sister of St. Frances and a student in pastoral counseling.

At the end of our one-year programs, we went our separate ways—she to take up a position at the International School of the Sacred Heart (ISSH) in Tokyo, and I back to teach in Aurora, Illinois. We promised to keep in touch but doubted we would see each other again. Before we parted, though, Vicky said, "Come visit me in Japan." I told her I was unlikely to do so because I harbored negative feelings about the Japanese, having lived as a child under the Japanese Occupation in China.

On the other hand, Vicky loved America. In her role as dean of studies at ISSH, she seized every opportunity to visit the United States. Wherever I moved, she promised, she would visit me. And she did.

In 1982 I picked her up at the Denver airport. As I carried her deceptively small but heavy bag up to my studio apartment, I asked, "Do you have gold bricks inside?"

"I have two slide carousels. I'm going to the University of Iowa for a job fair. I need to show these slides of my school to prospective teachers. Would you like to see them?" I agreed to do so. As I watched, strong memories returned of my years in Holy Ghost International School in my hometown of Qingdao.

Vicky told me she was looking for a school counselor. "Although we would prefer to hire a Sister of the Sacred Heart, I know you have all the qualifications for the job. Next year I will be headmistress. If it is possible, I'd love to offer you the job."

I told her I wanted to stay in Colorado and had sent out a dozen job applications in the area around Boulder and Denver. Appearing not to hear me, she continued, "When I get to Iowa, I'll send you an application, in case you change your mind."

After waiting in vain for positive responses to my job applications, I haphazardly filled out the ISSH application Vicky had sent me and mailed it. That spring I did manage to schedule three job interviews. The day before one of those interviews, which was for an adult counseling position, Vicky called and offered me the job in Japan. I told her about my upcoming interview. "Call me as soon as you find out," she said. I knew she had other candidates for the ISSH job.

At the time, I was working at a hospital switchboard. Nearby was a doctor's office. One day the doctor's secretary invited me into her office for a coffee break and brought out her *I Ching* book, which is the Chinese philosopher and poet Lao Tzu's book of oracles. She told me to think of a question and toss three coins. My thought was "Japan or not?" She looked up the code indicated by my coin toss and read, "The time of darkness is past. Winter is over. It is a turning point. Societies of people sharing the same views...."

I was reminded of my mother. Whenever she had to make a major decision, she would first consult the *I Ching*. Next she prayed. Then, with her eyes closed, she would open the *Bible* to a random page of the *Old Testament*, put a finger on the page, and read what was written. Then she would do the same with the *New Testament*. Finally, she would ask me about my most recent dream. (In China the dreams of young children are thought to have special meaning.)

When I got home I prayed over my *Bible*. My random selection in the *Old Testament* (Isaiah 43:9) was, "Let nations muster and assemble with every race." And from the *New Testament* (First Corinthians 16:19): All the churches of Asia send you greetings."

I closed the *Bible*, gave thanks, and shouted, "Yes!"

Vicky called the next day. She began to talk about the job description, salary, and currency exchange. I interrupted her and said, "Send me all that information in the mail. I'm coming. Just tell me when."

Her astonished reply was, "What! Did you say yes?"

Tokyo Bound

AFTER A 17-HOUR FLIGHT across the Pacific, I landed at Narita, the Tokyo/ Yokohama Airport. I realized I was regaining the time I'd lost when I crossed from Hong Kong to Seattle in 1949.

As I struggled with my luggage toward the crowd of people waiting to greet my fellow passengers, I was overjoyed to see my friend Vicky waving wildly. She had been waiting three hours, after a four-hour bus trip from the transit terminal in downtown Tokyo.

Shortly after we arrived at Vicky's home, she took me to see the apartment the school had provided for me on the third floor of a small building. The tiny kitchen had a table and two chairs. My bed was a futon in the middle of the tatami-covered floor in the living room. A reclining chair stood in the corner. Two doors opened to full-length closets, into one of which my bed would be stored during the day. A toilet next to a hot tub (or ofuro) and a small washing machine completed the amenities. A clothesline on the balcony served as a dryer. Basic dishes and utensils were stored in kitchen cabinets. Someone had intuited my wish for a simple life.

Next morning Vicky and I visited the school two blocks away, through the main gate of the University of the Sacred Heart. The International School was on the same campus. Before the end of World War II, the entire property had belonged to the Imperial Family. The Religious of the Sacred Heart (RSCJ) assumed ownership after the Japanese surrendered in 1945. The present empress had graduated from the University of the Sacred Heart.

Vicky took me to my office, marked "Guidance/Counseling" on the door. We entered and she outlined my responsibilities. I was to be available for personal counseling for students from kindergarten through grade 10. In addition I would be moderator of the high school social justice club, teach two mini courses in grade 10 and a religion class to grade 7. I would spend Wednesdays with students in kindergarten through grade 4.

When school opened at the end of August, I discovered that students came to ISSH from all over the world, and in an average year 75 countries were represented.

The language of instruction and communication was English. No other language was to be used while on campus. Many students began with no knowledge of English. We had English as a Second Language teachers from Australia, Canada, England, and the United States. Most students became proficient in English within a year.

Personally, I empathized with students who did not know English. At age 10, when I began Holy Ghost School, I had never heard of the ABCs, although my motivation to learn English was high. In Qingdao during the Japanese Occupation, learning the Japanese language was compulsory in my Chinese school. When I arrived in Japan to begin my new job, I secretly hoped I would somehow automatically remember the language I was coerced into learning. To my dismay, I remembered not a word! Learning an enemy's language by force had resulted in an automatic erasure effect. Fortunately, I could read a portion of the Japanese written language (kanji), because it was Chinese characters simplified.

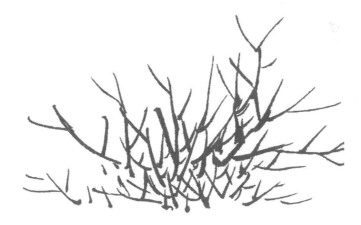

My Life in Japan

MY ORIGINAL CONTRACT with the International School of the Sacred Heart was from 1982 to 1984. Surprisingly, it took me very little time to overcome my resistance to working in Japan. I took a brief course in "Survival Japanese" and managed quite well on those rare occasions when it was necessary to converse in Japanese. Most people with whom I came in contact either spoke English or had some understanding of the language.

Every day was full of opportunities to stretch myself intellectually, socially, culturally, and professionally. Time passed quickly, and I kept renewing my contract. In the end, I stayed in Japan for 12 years. I made friends with faculty members and students from all over the world. Kazuko Suzuki, a teacher of Japanese in the foreign language department sought me out on several occasions and invited me to her home, although it was unusual for a near-stranger and foreigner to be invited to a Japanese home. She told me she wanted to heal the animosity between our two countries by building a bridge of friendship between us. Her husband Koji, a well-known family therapist, had published several books and was beginning to translate them into English. Both Kazuko and Koji had spent a year in the Divinity School at Yale University, and although he was quite fluent in English, Koji appreciated my help in translating his books.

The Suzukis became my family in Japan. I spent many weekends with them, enjoying Kazuko's cooking, in both traditional Japanese and Western cuisine. My friendship with the Suzukis has lasted for five decades.

Retirement Benefits… Or None

ONE DAY VICKY UY, who was now my headmistress, called me in to her office and asked, "Do know how much you have in your Social Security?" Although she was from the Philippines, and a Religious of the Sacred Heart, Vicky knew the school did not provide retirement benefits, and since I had been a Religious for 30 years, I had not built up any other such benefits. Nor did I own a home.

Following our conversation, I inquired about retirement benefits from my former Religious Community. I learned that because of the great exodus of Religious women since Vatican Council II, many sisters had no financial reserve to start a layperson's life. The Community did provide some funds to get started, but what they paid, retroactively, to Social Security was the minimum amount required to be eligible for Medicare. When I contacted the Social Security Office, I learned that if I were old enough to withdraw money at that time, I would receive $67 each month. I was then in my early 50s, but I doubted it would amount to enough to live on even 10 years later.

"Don't panic," I told myself. "I will just have to work longer. I could find a part-time job."

Teaching Conversational English

ONCE AGAIN I began to scan the want ads. In the English language news-paper I found an advertisement for a teacher of conversational English. The ad specified a preference for "American native speaker, Christian." Perfect. I made an appointment. After a brief interview I had the job and would start teaching two separate evening classes the following week, one on Tuesday and one on Friday, in Yokohama.

After working at ISSH on those days, I took the long train ride to Yokohama and back again to my apartment by 10 p.m. Although the streets in my residential district had few lights, I was not afraid to walk home in the dark. Japan had the lowest crime among the First World countries.

The students in one class were either university students or professionals. They could read English but could not speak the language.

The other class was housewives, and these students started learning English from the very beginning. For me, this was a perfect combination. I was learning about Japanese culture across the different layers of society. None of my students had been overseas. What they knew about Americans they had learned from movies and commercials.

Gradually some of them shed their custom of treating me as a teacher. They even stopped bowing their heads as they addressed me with the honorific title "sensei." I was able to go to the home of one student in the homemakers' class for a celebration of the lunar new year, and I attended the wedding of a student in the class of professionals. The bride, Rimiko, was a pharmacist. She had rejected the marriage her parents had arranged for her and married the man of her choice, an IBM worker. Rimiko and I kept up a correspondence after I left Japan. In 1988 Rimiko, her husband, and their children visited me at my home on Whidbey Island.

Southeast Asia

I SPENT MANY vacations during the years I was teaching and counseling at ISSH exploring the country and traveling around Southeast Asia. During my 1984 summer vacation, my good friend Jacques L'Heureux flew into Tokyo from Ottawa, Canada. After exploring Tokyo and Yokohama for a few days, we flew to Qingdao, China. At that time my sister Fung Ying and her husband were living there with their son, his wife and their four-year-old son. My nephew, Loon Shan (whose name means Dragon Mountain) made some of my favorite dishes and served delicious meals.

During the week we were there, we visited many places that were significant to me during my youth. I was now the tour guide for my friend, just as three years ago Fung Ying had been my guide.

After Qingdao, we went to Beijing, where Jacques was interested in even the smallest details. I was able to add some personal notes when we visited the Imperial Palace. My maternal grandfather had been a tutor of German for Empress Qing. She wanted to learn some German phrases so she could greet visiting dignitaries. (My grandfather had learned German when he studied to be a doctor of both Western and Eastern medicine.)

At the end of our travels in Japan and China, I asked Jacques for his impressions of the people. He said, "When we traveled in the trains in Japan, even though we were tightly packed together, no one ever made eye contact, and no words were exchanged. When we were in crowded buses in China, people stared at me until our eyes met. Most of the time they would gesticulate or use the few English words they knew, to get me to answer." These cultural differences reinforced our belief that our travels yielded the riches of cross-cultural friendship.

Thailand

IN 1985, December was an unusually cold month in Tokyo. Some of the kindergarten children at ISSH saw snow for the first time. When it came time to choose a spot for my winter vacation, I knew I wanted to go somewhere warm. I chose Thailand.

My first stop after landing in Bangkok was at a bank to exchange U.S. currency for baht. The clerk did not speak English. Before he could find a translator, though, I noticed that his business card included Chinese characters. Aha! He was of Chinese descent, and I discovered he spoke fluent Chinese. For the rest of my trip, I watched for people with whom I could speak in either Chinese or English.

I spent a portion of that trip traveling with an American couple I had met on the plane from Tokyo. We traveled to Koh Samui, a tiny island in the Tong Sai Bay of Thailand. While staying on Koh Samui we enjoyed the exotic cuisine, including fruits I had never even heard of before. After a week in that relaxing place, we traveled back to noisy, crowded Bangkok. As I flew back to Japan I felt reinvigorated and eager to begin the next school session at ISSH.

Taiwan

WHILE I WAS WORKING at ISSH, I learned that Sister George, who had been my third-grade teacher at St. Joseph School, was teaching in Taiwan. I lost no time in making contact with her. Coincidentally, she had learned that one of the children in her school was the grandchild of an aunt and uncle of mine. Big Aunt and Big Uncle had fled the Communists and followed Chiang Kai-shek, the leader of the nationalist government, to Taiwan in 1948. Through Sister George I learned that my aunt and uncle had died, but their son and his family were still there, and if I wanted to visit them she would try to help me find them.

Big Uncle, Sister George, Big Aunt in Taiwan

For my Christmas vacation in 1988, I flew to the Taipei airport in Taiwan to visit Sister George. She lived in a storeroom on one side of a church's choir loft. The room contained a metal bed, a chair, and a wooden stand. The stand served many purposes. It was a writing desk, a dining table, and a washstand. She did all her cooking on a small electric hotplate. On Sunday the two of us sat in the back pew of the church. When latecomers came in, they greeted Sister George and touched her. Her face radiated, and I knew she was living her heart's desire.

I took a train to meet my cousin in Taichung in central Taiwan. He ran to greet me, saying, "Siao mei mei (little younger sister)! You are as young as when I last saw you!" (The last time we had seen one another was four decades earlier.)

We did some sightseeing, and then my cousin and his wife drove me to pay our respects to my deceased aunt and uncle. He and I prayed over the tombs, and his wife brought paper gifts of clothing, gold bars, fruits, and other things, which she set on fire, in accordance with tradition.

We said a tearful good-bye at the airport. My cousin and I both knew this would probably be our last reunion.

Singapore

AT THE ISSH Family Festival in 1990, I won a round trip to Singapore on Singapore Airlines. My Christmas vacation destination was thus decided. Another ISSH teacher named Shirley, who was from Missouri, asked if she could pay her own way and travel with me.

Shirley's plane left a day ahead of mine, so we met in the hotel lobby the morning after I arrived in Singapore. I told her I had walked around the neighborhood of the hotel and stopped at a restaurant for a wonderful breakfast that featured food from several provinces in China. "Where did you eat breakfast yesterday?"

Shirley answered, "I walked to McDonald's. I love Egg McMuffins!"

(My niece, who lives in Hong Kong, had spent a year in Singapore. She said Singapore has the best authentic food of anywhere in the world. I knew I would not be wasting my calories on Egg McMuffins.)

Two of my former ISSH students drove us around the city and the surrounding countryside. We stopped at a park with food stalls that allowed Shirley to make choices that were, as she said, "at least recognizable."

The evening of our departure, Shirley agreed to go to an Indian restaurant, saying she had once eaten in an Indian restaurant in Chicago. Her hopes for a familiar type of meal were quickly dashed. Our plates were big banana leaves, and we had no eating utensils. Waiters brought us bowls of water and hand towels. Other waiters came bearing large platters of food from which we could choose. Everyone was eating with his or her fingers. Shirley had to choose between diving in and going hungry. Reluctantly, timidly, she ate.

As we flew back to Tokyo, I reflected on my experiences. Similar to my travels in other Southeast Asian countries, I savored the pleasure of learning a new culture, but my greatest pleasure was connecting and reconnecting with people.

Kwai Ling

FOR OUR SPRING holiday in 1982, I suggested to some friends that we vacation in Kwai Ling, a city in China I had never visited but had only heard and read about. I admit to having a financial reason to suggest a trip to a city in China.

I had inherited my family's home in Qingdao, which had been confiscated by the Communist government. Officially, the house was registered at the Bureau for Housing in my name. Deng Xiaoping had succeeded Mao, and the government was beginning to return properties to foreigners. The money I was to be given in payment for the house, however, was not to leave China. (I had put my nephew in charge of distributing the money so that he and my nieces could benefit. After we had determined we would go to Kwai Ling for a holiday, I contacted him and asked him to transfer the equivalent of $2000 to a bank in that city. My plan was that I would splurge and treat my friends to a fine time.)

When we arrived in Kwai Ling we took a walking tour around the city and stopped at the designated bank. "Very sorry, there is a delay," I was told. "Please come back tomorrow." After two more trips to the bank, I learned, "By mistake the money was sent back to Qingdao. It will take another week or so to get it back to this bank." So much for my "plan."

The next day we took a boat ride down the famous Lee River with its view of the mountains on the east bank. The view of the peaks through wisps of fog was reminiscent of famous Chinese silk screens. In my imagination I was in one such scroll, not just seeing it. I was reminded of the words of the ancient Chinese philosopher Chuang Tsu, "I was not sure if I were the butterfly or the setting."

When we went out into the countryside I thought I had gone back in time. Teams of oxen plowed the fields, and women bent between the rows gathering rice. It was a scene from a childhood storybook.

On our last day a young man came up and walked alongside us to practice his English. He explained he was an artist and his father had been an artist as well, and a famous one. "When my father tried to sell his scrolls during the Cultural Revolution, " he explained, "artists were disciplined. He was sent to the countryside for hard labor. I rescued some of his scrolls and hid them. Would you like to see them?"

He took us to his shabby apartment, which was nearby, and showed us the scrolls depicting beautiful scenes similar to what we had seen along the Lee River. I bought one of them and hung it on the wall of my apartment in Tokyo.

Psychic

INTERNATIONAL SCHOOLS did not always observe the American Thanksgiving holiday. Instead, they rotated holidays among the countries represented. In this rotation, 1982 was the year to celebrate Thanksgiving at ISSH in Tokyo, and Thursday and Friday would be school holidays.

Shortly before Thanksgiving, my friend Keb called to tell me about an extraordinary experience he had recently had with a psychic named Manfred, and to urge me to consult him. I told him I didn't really believe in psychics.

"I don't either," he replied, "but Manfred revealed something about my youth that explains what caused my present health problems. When I asked my sister about it, she told me what he said was true. Unfortunately, Manfred is so well known that before he even got to Tokyo his time was all booked up. Just in case he has an opening, though, here is his phone number."

I considered how unlikely it was that I would get an appointment, but because of my friendship with Keb, I decided to take a chance and call.

As it turned out, there had been a cancellation for Friday. If this had not been the year to celebrate American Thanksgiving, I would have been in school and unable to keep the appointment. Perhaps it was meant to be, I admitted to myself.

Manfred met me at the train station near his home. As we walked along together to his apartment, I told him nothing but my name. We sat at his kitchen counter, and he shuffled a pack of cards with strange pictures.

Without receiving any information from me, he told me the following things:

- You will be taking a trip overseas. (I had my ticket to fly to Seattle the following week.)
- You read a lot and are good with words.
- Your life has been very unusual.
- Your artistic expression is writing your life. It gives you much joy.
- You are involved in a lot of spirituality. Spiritual principles help you.

- The company where you are working is going through a lot of change. (I did not know at the time but after Christmas, the headmistress informed us of major changes in our course of studies, which would necessitate major staff changes.)
- I don't see you in a big city...a very nice country area...near an ocean... with many opportunities for hiking. (Later, after I met Kristine Marshall, we often hiked together in the Cascade and Olympic Mountains in Washington State.)

Before closing our session Manfred told me, "Your life's lesson is to love yourself. Don't be the aunt from overseas, always sending checks." At these last words, I almost fell off my stool. (The year before, there had been a major earthquake in San Francisco. The shop of my niece in that city was totally shattered, and I had sent her a check for $10,000.)

I still don't believe in ordinary psychics, but Manfred was extraordinary. Even though some of his statements might have applied to any number of people, everything he said to me was true, even though I didn't know some of it at the time.

U-Turn

MY CURRENT two-year contract with ISSH was due to end in June of 1984, but once again it could be renewed by mutual consent. I was beginning to think those two years might be enough. I decided to spend the summer vacation of 1983 traveling around Japan, since it might be my last holidays there. My friend Vicky suggested that she and I make a retreat in a Trappist Monastery in Hakodate, on Hokkaido, the northernmost island of Japan. That plan suited my yearning for a contemplative life.

Before we left for the monastery I prayed to be shown when to return to the United States. For eight days I had no hint. As we were getting ready to leave for our retreat, I was waiting for Vicky in the garden when my eyes fell on a tree with a two-foot trunk from which two branches reached up like arms. It reminded me of the symbol for a U-turn.

A few days into the retreat I had a dream that reinforced this thought. In the dream I was lost. I asked a young boy to help me find my way. He bent down and drew a shape on the sidewalk, saying, "Just turn at the corner, then turn again."

"God has a sense of humor," I thought when I awoke, but U-turn to where? I thought I heard an inner voice saying, "Keep on listening and seeing."

In regard to renewing my contract, Headmistress Vicky wanted to be notified before December if I decided I would not be back after the following June. She needed to know what vacancies there would be before going overseas in February to recruit teachers. Since I did not know what my next move should be, I renewed my contract for another year.

Genesis Farm

ONCE AGAIN, in 1984, I spent my summer vacation in the United States. During the last two weeks of that vacation I attended a workshop at Genesis Farm in New Jersey. Sister Miriam Terese, a Dominican nun, managed the farm. Her goal was to grow vegetables and animals based on sustainability principles. On Friday, the last day of the workshop, Marie Varely, one of the workshop participants asked me," Are you always going to live in Japan?"

I told her I would probably return to America one day, but that I didn't have a house or a place to live.

"What are your criteria for the choice of a place?" she asked. My list included the potential for meeting kindred spirits, a rural area close to nature but not far from a university and an airport, and near a body of water.

She interrupted my musing about my ideal home. "I know the perfect place for you. Chinook Learning Center on the grounds of the Whidbey Institute on Whidbey Island in Washington State." I had never heard of Chinook or Whidbey Island. "It's north of Seattle." Seattle was the city I had entered on first coming to the United States, but that was all I knew about it. I decided to check out her recommendation.

I arrived at the Mukilteo ferry dock at dusk on a Saturday in August. I inhaled the smell of saltwater, reminiscing about the many summers I had spent on the beach in Qingdao. My heart filled with joy on the ferry ride to Clinton.

A Chinook volunteer named Jim picked me up at the ferry. As he drove down a gravel lane on the tree-shaded grounds of the Whidbey Institute, I began to wonder if I was still on earth and not in heaven. When we arrived, only a farmhouse and a barn were visible. A guest house was down a slope. When I was taken to a place called Grannies, Jim said I could pick any room. No one was staying there because the Institute was between conferences. (During the summer they were usually booked solid, with no room for those who were just visiting.)

Once I was alone I sat on the deck. The sun was slowly slipping behind snow-covered peaks. In the distance I heard people chanting and someone strumming a guitar. The sound of drumming blended with the howl of a coyote.

When I got up the next morning, I noticed that above the entrance to my cottage was a horseshoe. Here was another object in the shape of a U!

On the first Sunday of every month a liturgy was held at the Institute. I was there on August 5, and the liturgy took place on the lawn in front of Grannies. All those in attendance sat on the lawn. Fritz Hull, founder of Chinook, and a former Jesuit priest, celebrated an ecumenical service, with the breaking of bread. There were readings from the *Bible*, poetry, and singing from different traditions. Someone danced. The service resonated within me.

After the liturgy we went to the farmhouse for a brunch featuring vegetables and fruit from the on-site organic garden. Fritz invited the newcomers to remain after the meal, and he showed slides of the history of Chinook. Around 3 p.m. everyone else left. I remained the sole inhabitant of 75 acres of wilderness.

The next day was Monday, and I had no schedule. I was to catch a plane to Portland, Oregon, on Tuesday for a connecting flight back to Tokyo. I wanted to travel around the island, but at that time Whidbey had no taxis or buses.

"Realtors!" I thought. "They drive people around." (Since I had been a nun for nearly all of my adult life, I knew nothing about buying property.) I called a realtor at random. Gary Martin, a Coldwell-Banker realtor, drove me to spectacular sites, several with panoramic views. "Before I take you back to the ferry," he said, "I need to stop at my office to put my papers together."

As I stood in his office in Clinton, my conscience caught up with me. I had taken three hours of this man's time with no intention of buying property. I said, "Gary, if I were interested in one of the lots you showed me, what do I have to do?"

"All you have to do is write me a check for $500 as earnest money," he said. I wrote a check and put it on his desk.

The next day while I waited in Portland for the jet that would take me back to Tokyo, reality dawned on me. What had I done? I had agreed to buy a piece of land in the middle of nowhere. I didn't know anyone there. Nor did I know how they lived. They may all be farmers.

I picked up the pay phone and called Gary. "I'm sorry. I don't know what came over me. Please tear up that check."

Gary answered calmly. "It's not a problem. If you change your mind and want to go ahead with the purchase, you have my business card. Just contact me." I never felt more relieved.

Next day, when I arrived back at ISSH, I stopped at Vicky's office and told her my story. "Don't ever let me loose again. I do stupid things," I said.

"It may be the smartest financial step you ever made," she replied. "My Chinese father, who was an immigrant to Manila, told me that we Chinese save money in gold or land. You will need a house when you go back to the States. You could sell the land and pay for property wherever you choose to live." I took her advice. Right there in her office I called Gary.

"If you have torn up my check, I'll mail you another one."

"It's still under my phone," he said. By the end of the next school year I had paid for the property in full, $20,000 for one-third of an acre. I filed the sale and the title document and thought I could dismiss this purchase from my mind. I soon discovered, however, that I had to pay property tax twice a year and that I was entitled to be a voter of Washington State.

From then on, every summer when I returned to North America for visits with my friends and family. I usually spent a week at Chinook Learning Center, participating in a conference or workshop. Gradually, Kay Metcalf, the receptionist, became my friend. Only in retrospect did I realize this had been my U-turn.

God's ways are mysterious.

Farewell to Japan

SEVERAL MORE YEARS passed before I could make my "U-turn" a reality. It was not easy to bring my job at ISSH to a close and sever my connections to the people I had grown to know and love. By 1994, when I finally left Japan, I had been working and living in that country for 12 years.

I made a list of things to do in my office, what to discard and what to keep for my successor. As I emptied my box of business cards, printed with "Ms. Gloria Chou, Director of Guidance and Counseling, International School of the Sacred Heart, Tokyo, Japan," I had a lump in my throat. These cards summarized my identity. From that time on I would be without a title or a position.

On the other hand, after 40 years as an educator and having to report to one authority figure or another, I would finally be free to be fully myself.

Bidding farewell to the ISSH faculty and students was actually not too difficult, because the school population was transient and always changing. My friends were another matter. I had become very strongly attached to the Suzuki family and to members of my two English conversation classes. (Both classes had sayonara parties in my honor and showered me with gifts.)

I made short work of packing up my apartment. The school paid for sending my belongings to my next residence. Since I didn't own a home I did not keep much in the way of belongings. My friend Mary Wilson, at Sojourners House in Seattle, where I had spent several summers as a volunteer, offered to store my things for me until I was settled.

On June 9, 1994, I departed from Japan and looked forward to a summer of adventure in Europe followed by a new life ahead in America.

Travels Around Europe

I HAD PROMISED several of my friends who lived in Europe that I would return to America by way of Europe and would visit them en route.

My long-time friend Alinda (Lindy) met me in Geneva, Switzerland. Although we had not seen one another for eight years, it seemed no time at all had passed as we resumed our friendship. Lindy and her husband lived in a chalet in the foothills of the Swiss Alps, with a view of the Matterhorn from her balcony. We also saw cattle as they moved down from the hills, bells swinging from leather straps around their necks. Lindy and her husband were Christian Science missionaries in the nearby village of Lausanne. Year-round skiing was a side benefit of their job

From Switzerland a fast train took me to Paris, where Jacques was waiting to meet me. He had come to France from Ottawa to bless the wedding of his friend Francois who had made reservations for us at a hotel near the Louvre. Francois took us to dinner in a cozy restaurant on the Champs Elysees. Jacques and I traveled by train to the Cathedral at Chartres, the one place I had really set my heart on visiting. When I stepped into the immense space and into the center of the Labyrinth, which was built in the 13th century, my whole body trembled. Replicas of this labyrinth have been created all over the world, including at the Whidbey Institute on Whidbey Island.

England was my next destination. Margaret Moorhead, a Religious of the Sacred Heart of Jesus, had been a colleague on the ISSH faculty. She showed me the highlights of London, including tickets to *Les Miserables,* with its original cast, and tea at the Ritz Hotel, built in 1906 and considered by many to be the world's finest hotel.

Another friend from ISSH, Beth Mooy flew to England from her home in Michigan. We drove around the British countryside and crossed over to the Holy Island of Lindisfarne.

Beth and I traveled together to Yorkshire, where another former ISSH colleague lived. The Yorkshire lifestyle was quite a contrast to London, and Beth and I agreed that folks in the countryside were much more hospitable and friendly.

At the end of the European trip Beth and I parted ways, and I flew to Minnesota where I was welcomed by my friend Jim Fournier and his wife Karen. Jim had been my most compatible teammate in campus ministry at St. Mary's University. Jim and Karen came to visit me many times when I was in the Puget Sound area of Washington State.

How good it was to reconnect with old friends. And how exciting to head onward, to my temporary home in the United States, Sojourners House, in Seattle, Washington.

My Journey to Whidbey Island

NEAR A CATHOLIC Church in the University District in Seattle stood a housing complex that had been intended for novitiates but was not being used. Sister Mary Wilson, a Sister of Providence, had suggested that the buildings be used for housing for women who had been incarcerated and were in need of a place to live. She proposed to call the residence Sojourners House.

There were 12 rooms upstairs in the facility, each with a sink, as well as two larger rooms for staff members. Sister Mary invited me to stay in one of the staff rooms in return for providing counseling services. I was grateful to have a place to stay in Seattle as a temporary home and somewhere to store my belongings from my Tokyo apartment.

Prospective residents of Sojourners were carefully screened and had to agree to abide by rules such as the following:
- They must either have a day job or be in training for one.
- Alcohol was forbidden on the premises.
- They must behave in a respectful manner to one another, to staff, and to the facility itself.
- They could watch television only after dinner.
- If they broke any of the rules (such as drinking or behaving violently) they had to leave.
- They must be present for at least three community meals a week and help prepare one of those meals.

After a period of time during which they behaved responsibly and showed the ability to be independent, they were given assistance in moving to an apartment. Each resident was assigned a staff member as her counselor and support person. I was one of those counselors.

On my days off I usually went to the Japanese Park in the Arboretum and sat in its pavilion. A resident heron often came close enough to help me clear the negative energies I carried from Sojourners. At other times I stayed in a rented apartment on Whidbey Island, near the property I had purchased. Someone heard I owned a lot and recommended that I contact Carl Magnusson as a prospective builder. I learned Carl Magnusson was actually neither a professional contractor nor an architect. He was an artist who did building jobs to support his family.

A rainbow over my new house ... a good sign

My House on Simmons Drive

WHEN WE MET, Carl and I resonated immediately. At our first meeting he interviewed me to get to know my interests, my values, myself. My tiny house (only 640 square feet) has often been described as a sculpture, a work of art. Incorporated into it is a totem pole carved by another local artist named Pat McVay. It features a rising phoenix, a representation of my name.

Oneness was the theme of my house—oneness with nature, between East and West, spirit and matter, across many cultures. The placement of the house, as well as its design, followed the principles of Feng Shui. It was a simple home that provided for the health of the mind, body, and spirit.

Although I had agreed to live and work at Sojourners for two years, my health and spirit were beginning to be affected by the negativity of the

Interior view and Rising Phoenix totem

residents, so following my fortuitous meeting with Carl, I decided to leave Sojourners after only one year.

Another fortunate coincidence occurred when I met a woman who was selling her land and needed to get rid of a 32-foot trailer. I had the trailer moved to my land, and Carl connected water and septic systems so the trailer could become my temporary home, until I could move into the only "real" home I ever owned. Meanwhile, since I lived on-site, I was available to run errands, clean up the building site, and stain the cedar shingles.

On June 1, 1995, the building site was excavated. On June 25, the birthday of both Carl Magnusson and myself, we dedicated the site to the spirit of my parents. I moved in to my beautiful new home on October 1, 1995.

A Stroke ... Almost

EARLY IN JUNE, 2010, two weeks before my 79th birthday, I experienced blurred vision in my left eye. It was a frightening experience, and I sought medical help right away. After an MRI, Dr. Liu, a neurologist, told me, "Your blurred vision was caused by a burst capillary in the right occipital portion of your brain. You were lucky. You could have had a full stroke." And then she ordered further tests.

Before the date when I was scheduled to have the tests, I sent Dr. Liu this message: "Please keep in mind my approach to health as you consider the next steps following the results of the two tests I will undergo today. I have never had major surgeries, nor have I taken prolonged prescription drugs. Whatever the tests show, I will not accept radical treatments, e.g. surgery, radiation, chemotherapy. I request that you recommend for me gentle ways of sustaining my life. I prefer to die with dignity rather than resort to invasive ways of prolonging life."

Cristwood Park

I CONSIDERED my near-stroke as a wake-up call. My two good friends, Elisa and Kristine, were familiar with my philosophy and my health directive. Together they swung into action. Over the next several months they drove me around to visit several senior residences in the Puget Sound area. Meanwhile, I got busy on the internet, searching out facilities that would meet my needs. Cristwood Park met most of my criteria. It is in the Shoreline district of North Seattle, about a 30-minute drive from Whidbey Island. It has a woodland setting, with trails among the trees around the campus. Approximately 150 residents live in the independent community at Cristwood. The facility provides opportunities for intergenerational activities.

Although I was in no hurry to leave Whidbey Island and the only house I ever owned, I wanted to make this last major transition while I could still organize the move. And I wanted to be alert enough to develop new relationships and participate in activities in my new home.

My friend Lois had recently terminated her lease on an apartment in Langley on Whidbey Island and was looking for a new place to rent. I suggested she consider renting my house, and she readily agreed, although she needed to vacate her apartment by July 1.

Spurred on by Lois's schedule, as well as my having settled on Cristwood Park as my best choice of residence, I decided to make the move immediately. The first night I slept at Cristwood Park was June 28, 2011, just over one year after my "almost" stroke.

Happy landing!

My Life at Cristwood

LEARNING THE NAMES of my 150 new "neighbors" at Cristwood posed a daunting challenge. In fact, I realized I would never be able to know them all. After a while, I began to notice most residents merely greeted each other by saying, "Hello, how are you?" Some even passed one another with downcast eyes. For me, that was not enough.

I wanted to make deeper and wider connections with people. After consulting with the management of the facility, I initiated a bi-monthly "conversation café." Among the individuals who attended those meetings I found a few kindred spirits with whom I am still in contact.

From my first days at Cristwood, I had felt drawn to eat at a table where an elderly man sat, often alone. Wesley Wahls and I began to discuss topics of common interest. We continued our conversations over the telephone, with book recommendations and the sharing of newsworthy anecdotes.

After some time, Wes suffered a minor stroke, which forced a move to the skilled nursing facility on the upper campus at Cristwood. Every afternoon I walked up to visit him, and we continued our chats.

One day he pulled my hand closer and said, "I think we're soul mates. I don't really know what that is, but I feel wonderful." I'm sure he was lonely following his wife's death not long before he moved to Cristwood.

I held his hand and explained, "Wes, you met my friend Jacques, when he flew more than 2,000 to visit me. He is also my soul mate."

Wes died a week later. I have his photo on my nightstand so I can continue our conversations.

Hospital Stay

IN THE MIDDLE of November, 2014, I began to feel tired all the time. When I told Dr. Catherine Smith, my primary care physician, about my unremitting fatigue, she immediately sent me to the hospital, where I spent a week undergoing various tests. I was poked and prodded, gave blood samples, and experienced X-rays and biopsies.

Finally, the diagnosis was handed down. I suffered from adenocarcinoma of the lungs, a type of cancer that frequently afflicts older women who have never smoked. Throughout my uncomfortable ordeal in the hospital, I experienced extraordinary kindness from caregivers, and especially from Dr. Smith and my friend Kristine. Since I have always believed I was born to learn certain lessons, this was an important lesson for me: Love crosses all barriers.

In a consultation following the diagnosis, Dr Smith told me about three options available to me: 1. Surgery; 2. Radiation or chemotherapy; and 3. Hospice and palliative care. I chose the last of the three. In my health-care directive I had indicated that if ever I became unable to care for myself and was nearing the end of my life I would like to be taken care of in a facility such as Saratoga View Adult Home in Langley, on Whidbey Island, a private hospice facility operated by Dr. Grethe Cammermeyer.

True to the theme of opportunities arising quickly in my life, one of the three patient rooms at Saratoga View suddenly became available. My good friend Colette from Cristwood Park drove me to visit the facility and inspect the available room, which has a view across Saratoga Passage on Puget Sound to Gedney Island. In moving to Saratoga View I would be returning to Whidbey Island, where I had lived for 15 years.

Colette said, "Even though I will miss you, this is the perfect place for you." I signed up immediately and moved within a few days, with extremely generous help from my good friends on Whidbey. My deepest gratitude goes out to each of them—Kristine and Boyd, Elisa and Norm. Now it is time to focus on my next lesson: Letting go.

Letting Go

AND SO HERE I am at Saratoga View Adult Home, in these beautiful sur-roundings on Whidbey Island, often visited by long-time friends and just as frequently contacted by loved ones near and far away. I am very well cared for; I want for nothing. I have loved my life; I love it still.

Writing this memoir has allowed me to revisit all the stages of my life, the people I have known and loved, and the lessons I have learned throughout my journey. I have spent much time and energy selecting what to take with me and what to leave behind.

Now, as I approach the end of my life and complete the learning of my life's lessons, I hope I have understood those lessons well and am ready for the final letting-go.

This is the last chapter. I will leave this story behind with you.

"Into thy hands I commend my spirit."

Acknowledgements

AS THE END of my life comes into sight, my fervent wish is to see my memoir in print. Because she understood that wish, Sara Benum, my long-time friend, agreed to be my editor. I thank her for her energy in setting deadlines for both of us, for her expertise, and most of all, because she could almost read my thoughts and my soul, for her ability to describe me better than I could have done myself.

I deeply appreciate Grethe Cammermeyer for her support, and especially in making up for my poor computer skills.

I thank Pat Cochran, who spent many Tuesdays holding "story sharing class."

Thank you to Betty Freeman, patient messenger and compassionate friend throughout the process of this project.

Thanks also to Marion Blue, who was my writing teacher and strongly encouraged me to keep writing, even for publication.

And thanks to all those who patiently or politely listened to my many stories.